Patriarch

Notes of
an Expert Witness

Phyllis Chesler

Common Courage Press   Monroe Maine

Library of Congress Cataloguing-in-Publication Data
Chesler, Phyllis.
Patriarchy : notes of an expert witness / Phyllis Chesler.
p. cm.
Includes Index.
ISBN 1-56751-039-6 (cloth). -- ISBN 1-56751-038-8 (paper)
1. Women's rights--United States--Case studies. 2. Women--
United States--Social conditions--Case studies. 3. Power (Social
sciences)--United States--Case studies. 4. Feminism--United States.
I. Title. HQ1421.C49   1994   94-21995
   305.42'0973--dc20   CIP

Common Courage Press
P.O. Box 702
Monroe, ME 04951
207-525-0900
fax: 207-525-3068

First Printing

Contents

Acknowledgments

I am grateful to Flic Shooter and Greg Bates of Common Courage Press, and to the following people for their loving support: my exceedingly resourceful mother, Lillian; my dear friend and publisher Merle Hoffman; my ever-efficient assistant, Melissa Slaybaugh; my former housekeeper, Sharon Smalls-Bey; my dedicated and skillful acupuncturist, Helene Kostre; my inspired nutritionist, Nicole Janssen, my ever-reliable chiropractor, Harvey Rossell; my sympathetic internist, Susan Levine; and my editor Ronni Sandroff. And to Ilana Rubenfeld and Susan Bender—for everything.

I dedicate this book to all those who will continue the work of feminist revolution, and to the coming generations.

Introduction

Heroism Is Our Only Alternative

It is an honor and a joy to have these articles issued in book form by Common Courage Press. The articles span an eight-year period, from 1986 to 1994.

In only 25 years, a visionary feminism has managed to seriously challenge, if not transform, world consciousness. Nevertheless, I am saddened and sobered by the realization that no more than a handful of feminists have been liberated from the lives of grinding poverty, illness, overwork, and endless worry that continue to afflict most women and men in America.

Before I introduce the articles, let me introduce myself. I am the woman who, in 1970, nearly a quarter of a century ago, demanded one million dollars in reparations—a token sum—from the assembled members of the American Psychological Association on behalf of all those women who had never been helped by the mental health professions but who had, in fact, been further abused: punitively labeled, ordered to "adjust" to their lives as second and third class citizens and blamed when they failed to do so, overly tranquilized, sexually seduced while in treatment, hospitalized, often against their will, given shock and insulin coma therapy or lobotomies, strait-jacketed both physically and chemically, and used as slave labor in state mental asylums. "Maybe the newly formed Association for Women in Psychology could set up an alternative to a mental hospital with the money," I suggested, "or a shelter for runaway wives."

Two thousand of my colleagues were in the audience; they seemed shocked. Many laughed. Loudly. Nervously. Some looked embarrassed, others relieved. Quite obviously, I was "crazy." Afterwards, someone told me that jokes had been made about my "penis envy." Friends: this was 1970—not 1870. And I was a colleague, on the platform and at the podium.

I went home and wrote *Women and Madness*, which I published in 1972. The book, and I, were embraced, instantly, by other feminists, both male and female, and by many women in general. However, my analysis of how diagnostic labels were used to stigmatize women and of why more women than men were involved in "careers" as psychiatric patients, was either ignored or treated as a passing sensation by those in positions of power within the psychiatric and psychological professions.

Women and Madness has remained in print ever since, and has been cited often in the professional journals. Although feminist views have influenced the theory and practice of mental health in vital ways, feminist views within the mental health establishment have mainly been marginalized, ignored, sometimes debated, and essentially "disappeared." Despite some noteworthy exceptions, radical feminists and radical feminist views have not shaped what most graduate, nursing, medical, counseling, social work, and pastoral students learn.

My generation of feminists hit the ground running. We had a sense of collective destiny and invulnerability that now seems naive—and extraordinarily privileged. For the first time in our lives, *we—and our analysis of reality*, became the center of our universe. Feminists had (psychologically) declared that Man as woman's God on earth was dead—easily the equivalent of men's earlier political, scientific, and philosophical declarations that God and King were dead.

Despite our considerable training as "Daddy's girls," we married History and each other. We wanted revolutionary transcendence, and justice, more than we wanted romantic (incestuous) love, individual solutions, or careers. Actually, we were Americans, and we wanted it all, but we'd been hungry for sisterhood in the service of *heroism* all our lives. Some of us found more—and some found less—sisterhood and brotherhood than we'd dreamed possible; but, for a while, we lived extraordinary lives. We did not transform the world— although it is a different world today than when we first started out. Every inch of consciousness, dignity, and institutional control had to be fought for; that fight continues. Despite our willingness to make sacrifices, many of us were still silenced, our work "disappeared" or stolen and watered down, our collective resistance rendered invisible, our ability to teach the next generations savagely curtailed.

I became—and have remained—a liberation psychologist, a radical political and spiritual activist, an academic researcher who loves myths and tales, and who refuses to teach or write in an obfuscated, Mandarin language. In *Women and Madness*, and in all my subsequent books and articles, I was charting the psychology of human beings in captivity, who, as a caste, did not control the means of production or reproduction. I was trying to understand what a struggle for freedom might entail, psychologically and politically, when the colonized group was female. Better orgasms or token positions of privilege, racism, homophobia, and woman-hating in female, or feminist, voices wasn't good enough. Early on, I began talking about a feminist government in exile. How else, I asked, could we airlift women and children out of Bangladesh or Bosnia, i.e., out of patriarchy?

For a long time now, like many others, I've been a minister without portfolio, representing that nonexistent government.

From 1971 to 1991, I routinely received—and dealt with—50 to 75 calls and letters *a week* from women in crisis, and at least 75 to 100 requests *per week* to sign petitions, form organizations, attend meetings, demonstrations, press conferences, read and comment on manuscripts, appear on television, talk to newspapers, meet with visiting feminist dignitaries, lobby legislatures, coordinate fundraisers, etc.—all unpaid activities. My office away from the university was busy, and costly. Subsidizing my intellectual and feminist activism became more difficult as paid lectures dried up for all but a few radical feminists during the "backlash" 1980s.

Although I received tenure in the mid-1970s, and, courtesy of a class action lawsuit on behalf of women, was in 1990, finally promoted to the rank of (Full) Professor, I have never been granted the opportunity to teach graduate students or supervise doctoral dissertations. I have been unable to train the next generations *personally*, to take pleasure in their company and in their triumphs, to support them in battle, to make common cause. However, perspective is everything: Most radical feminists of my generation were never hired in the first place.

Now, onward—at least to the pieces you're about to read.

Three of these pieces were first published in *On The Issues* magazine: "Feminism and Illness" in 1992; "Marcia Rimland's Deadly Embrace" in 1993; and "A Wolf in Feminist Clothing" in 1994. The long piece on the Aileen Wuornos case first appeared in *On The Issues*, too, in two installments, in 1992 and 1993, although for political reasons I decided to expand and transform the material into a series of academic legal articles. The first two such articles appeared in *The St. John's Law Review* and in *The Criminal Practice Law Report*, both in 1993.

Introduction

The remaining articles in this collection have appeared in a variety of places: I wrote "Women of the Asylum" as an Introduction to an anthology of women's first-person accounts of their psychiatric hospitalizations in America from 1840 to 1945, edited by Jeffrey Geller and Maxine Harris; it was originally to be published by the American Psychiatric Association Publication Society, but was, instead, published by Doubleday-Anchor in 1994.

"Mothers on Trial: Custody and the Baby M Case" was originally a speech I delivered at a conference at the NYU Law School in 1987 and later published in 1990, as part of the conference proceedings in a volume edited by Dorchen Leithold and Janice Raymond, titled *The Sexual Liberals and the Attack on Feminism*, and published by The Athene Series, Pergamon Press.

"The Men's Auxiliary: Protecting the Rule of the Fathers" first appeared in *Women Respond to the Men's Movement*, the anthology edited by Kay Leigh Hagan, and published by Harper Collins in 1992.

Three years ago, when I became ill with Chronic Fatigue Immune Dysfunction Syndrome, I realized that, absent a serious commitment from a major university or foundation, I might have to stop my work in the world. I haven't, of course. I've simply become a citizen of a "Third World" country: I'm slower, deeper, less impatient, less high-speed, more philosophical, and more appreciative of the so-called "small" things: good weather, good friends, good literature, sex, the ocean, solitude; I am *more*, not less, committed to radical visions of reality.

Being ill and temporarily disabled made me more outraged by the contempt and indifference with which most sick and disabled/differently-abled people are treated in our country. "Feminism and Illness", the fifth piece here, has occasioned the most extraordinary response; women, and some men, have called, written, wept, and thanked me for speaking for them, for "telling it like it is."

The themes of *Women and Madness* are, unfortunately, not out of date. Psychiatric labels and diagnoses—the *institution* of psychiatry, is still used to stigmatize traumatized populations of second-class citizens, *and* to punitively diagnose all those who dare to rebel. When women allege they've been sexually harassed and/or discriminated against on the job in other vital ways, incredibly, they are still forced into psychiatric exams, and treated as if they, the victims, are "crazy."

Hard to believe? What about the women in the military who "complained" about being sexually harassed, *post* Tailhook, and who'd been punished for doing so? In 1994, the women testified before the House Armed Services Committee that once they'd filed grievances, they were ostracized, brutally questioned about their private sex lives, transferred to dead-end jobs, and forced out of the armed services.[1] In addition, Lieutenant Darlene Simmons, a Navy lawyer, had been ordered to take a psychiatric exam after she accused her commander of harassment in 1991 and 1992. A psychiatric exam? How absurd, how chilling, how familiar.

And what about Dr. Margaret Jensvold, winner of a prestigious fellowship at the National Institutes of Mental Health (NIH), and a psychiatrist, who was "advised" to see a psychotherapist by her allegedly sexist supervisor, Dr. David Rubinow, if she wished to stay at NIH. Dr. Jensvold is now the *second* female psychiatrist at NIH in the last five years who has filed a lawsuit charging sex discrimination; according to Dr. Jean Hamilton, Jensvold's immediate predecessor who settled an EEOC complaint against the superviser, women researchers are routinely called names like "Witch," "Wicked Bitch," "Booby Lady" and, more benignly, "Sugar."

Double standards of mental illness still prevail. John Wayne(!) Bobbitt wasn't diagnosed or convicted as "insane" for raping and beating his wife; Lorena Bobbitt wasn't diagnosed as "insane" for *staying* with her tormenter and torturer. She was convicted of "insanity" only for trying to get the pain to stop and, of course, for taking the weapon away from the offender.

Richard Mallory, the john who brutally raped Aileen Wuornos, who had previously been jailed for attempted rape, was not presented to the jury as an "insane," woman-hating criminal. Wuornos was portrayed as "crazy" for having fought and killed in self-defense; perhaps she was also seen as "crazy" because she was a prostitute, and a lesbian, and despite all the violence she'd absorbed, hadn't had the decency to kill herself but had, instead, dared to turn the rage outward, against men.

William and Betsy Stern were not seen as "crazy" for signing a surrogacy contract or for having Baby M's mother arrested for running away with that child; only Mary Beth Whitehead was seen as "crazy," "borderline," "narcissistic," and as an "unfit" mother(!), for wanting to keep the child she'd given birth to and had been breast-feeding for four months.

Marcia Rimland's ex-husband was not suspected or convicted of incestuous insanity when he abused his wife and (allegedly) sexually abused his four-year-old daughter. Marcia Rimland was the "crazy" one, because she'd dared to expose the abuse, tried to get the system to "protect" her and her daughter and, when it failed to do so, because she took matters into her own hands and killed herself and her daughter—to get the abuse to stop.

Some say that men are getting gentler, more "sensitive," more in touch with their feelings—and with where the diapers are. This is true, for some men. However, are men in the forefront of the battle against violence against women? Have men stopped raping and gang-raping and battering and verbally abusing women and children? Have a sufficient number of men stopped sexually enslaving and/or buying women and children? Do men no longer sexually harass women on the job—or keep them out of the clubhouse altogether? Are women no longer impoverished, either economically or spiritually, by patriarchy? Have serial killers called it a day?

Women—and men—are punitively labeled for deserting their sex-role stereotypical behavior. (Recently, I've begun to document that women are sentenced more harshly for committing so-called "male" crimes than men are.) This is a hard lesson to learn: that "bad" things happen to us—simply because we're ourselves, or whistle blowers about what happens to people for being themselves, and/or for failing that privilege. It's mind-boggling, enraging. It either turns us into apologists for patriarchy—or into feminists: not the "fun" kind.

Some say that the feminist voice is now widespread, persistent, and difficult to resist. I agree. However, I am also very aware that patriarchy systematically "disappeared" radical feminist thought and activism for the last three hundred years. It's what's already happened in my own lifetime to the work of the major radical feminist thinkers and activists of my generation.

I ask: What can we do to combat the erosion of feminist gains in each and every generation? College-level women's studies classes are important, but that's rather late in the day to start counteracting what people have already been learning all their lives. Unfortunately, we have no way of preserving and continuously transmitting our consciousness to successive generations. Without infrastructure—without lasting, structural vehicles, what we know dies out with us. And future generations are condemned to reinvent the feminist wheel.

But aren't feminists quoted all the time in the media now? Don't we have countless Women's Studies programs and courses? Aren't the "badwhitemen" on the run, defeated by the proponents of "politically correct," multicultural world-views? Ah, not exactly. Most feminist academic programs, like the most quoted feminists, are not radical; are, indeed, like high fashion models and prostituted women, omnipresent, visible, *precisely* because they do not seriously threaten the status quo.

Women's survival (and for that matter, men's survival too) and health depend on our doing many things simultaneously on a "number of levels." Freedom and justice do wonders for one's mental health!

So, as Freud once asked: "What do women want?" For starters, and in no particular order: freedom, food, nature, shelter, leisure, freedom from violence, justice, music, non-patriarchal family, poetry, community, independence, books, physical/sexual pleasure, education, solitude, the ability to defend ourselves, love, ethical friendships, theater and the arts, health, dignified employment, political comrades, support during chronic or life-threatening illness. Women and men need all this and more—and not just when we're in severe psychological or physical pain, but always, as a way of life, because we're human beings.

I've been envisioning a sovereign feminist government for a long time and that vision guides me still.

Phyllis Chesler
Brooklyn, New York
March, 1994

NOTES

1. Simmons has since been reinstated.

Women of the Asylum

First-Person Accounts of Women
Hospitalized in American Psychiatric
Institutions 1840–1945

"Women of the Asylum" is a true companion volume to my own *Women and Madness*, first published in 1972. These 27 first-person accounts are lucid, sometimes brilliant, always heartbreaking, and utterly principled, even heroic. Incredibly, these women were not broken or silenced by their lengthy sojourns in Hell. They bear witness to what was done to them and to those less fortunate than themselves who did not survive the brutal beatings, the near-drownings, the force-feedings, the body-restraints, the long periods in their own filth and in solitary confinement, the absence of kindness or reason—which passed for "treatment." These historical accounts brought tears to my eyes.

Whether these women of the asylum were entirely sane, or whether they had experienced post-partum or other depressions, heard voices, were "hysterically" paralyzed, or disoriented; whether the women were well-educated and well-to-do, or members of the working poor; whether they had led relatively privileged lives or had been beaten, raped, abandoned, or victimized in other ways; whether the women accepted or could no longer cope with their narrow social roles; whether they had been idle for too long or had worked too hard for too long and were fatigued beyond measure— none were treated with any kindness or medical or spiritual expertise.

Elizabeth T. Stone (1842) of Massachusetts describes the mental asylum as "a system that is worse than slavery"; Adriana Brinckle (1857) of Pennsylvania describes the asylum as a "living death," filled with "shackles," "darkness," "handcuffs, straight-jackets, balls and chains, iron rings and…other such relics of barbarism"; Tirzah Shedd (1862) tells us: "This is a wholesale slaughter house…more a place of punishment than a place of cure"; Clarissa Caldwell Lathrop (1880) of New York writes: "We could not read the invisible inscription over the entrance, written in the heart's blood of the unfortunate inmates, 'Who enters here must leave all hope behind.'" Female patients were routinely beaten, deprived of sleep, food, exercise, sunlight, and all contact with the outside world, and were sometimes even murdered. Their resistance to physical (and mental) illness was often shattered. Sometimes, the women tried to kill themselves as a way of ending their torture.

I am amazed, and saddened, that I was able to complete my formal education *and* write *Women and Madness* without knowing more than a handful of the stories gathered here.

In 1969, I helped found the Association for Women in Psychology (AWP). I was a brand-new Ph.D., a psychotherapist-in-training, an Assistant Professor, and a researcher. Inspired by the existence of a visionary and radical grassroots feminist movement, I was conducting a study on women's experiences as psychiatric and psychotherapeutic patients, and on sex-role stereotyping in psychotherapeutic theory and practice. I planned to present some preliminary findings at the annual convention of the American

Psychological Association (APA) in 1970, in Miami.

I read psychiatric, psychological, and psychoanalytic texts, and historical, mythological, and fictional accounts of women's lives. I located the stories of European women who'd been condemned as witches (including Regine Pernoud's account of Joan of Arc) and, from the sixteenth century on, psychiatrically diagnosed and imprisoned. I read the nineteenth century American heroine, Elizabeth Packard (whose words are contained here), and about some of Freud's patients, most notably: Anna O (who became the feminist crusader Bertha Pappenheim) and Dora, whose philandering and syphilitic father, in Freud's words, "had handed [Dora] over to [a] strange man in the interests of his own [extra-marital] love-affair."

I learned that some well-known and accomplished women, Zelda Fitzgerald, Virginia Woolf, Frances Farmer, Sylvia Plath, and the fictionally named "Ellen West," had been psychiatrically labeled and hospitalized. Based on numerous statistical, academic, and case studies, and on interviews with female ex-mental and psychotherapy patients, I began to document what patriarchal culture and consciousness had been doing to women for thousands of years, including psychiatrically and "therapeutically," in the twentieth century in the United States. I was also charting the psychology of human beings in captivity, who, as a caste, did not control the means of production or reproduction and who were routinely abused and shamed sexually, economically, politically, and socially. I was trying to understand what a struggle for freedom might entail, both politically and psychologically, when the colonized group was female.

In the midst of this work, I attended the 1970 APA convention. Instead of delivering an academic paper on behalf of AWP, I asked the assembled APA members for one million dollars "in reparations" for those women who had never been helped by the mental health professions but who had, in fact, been further abused: punitively labeled, ordered to "adjust" to their lives as second and third class citizens and blamed when they failed to do so, overly tranquilized, sexually seduced while in treatment, hospitalized, often against their will, given shock and insulin coma therapy or lobotomies, strait-jacketed both physically and chemically, and used as slave labor in state mental asylums. "Maybe AWP could set up an alternative to a mental hospital with the money," I suggested, "or a shelter for runaway wives."

Two thousand of my colleagues were in the audience; they seemed shocked. Many laughed. Loudly. Nervously. Some looked embarrassed, others relieved. Quite obviously, I was "crazy." Afterwards, someone told me that jokes had been made about my "penis envy." Friends: this was 1970—not 1870. And I was a colleague, on the platform and at the podium.

Women and Madness was first published in 1972. It was embraced, instantly, by other feminists and by many women in general. However, my analysis of how diagnostic labels were used to stigmatize women and of why more women than men were involved in "careers" as psychiatric patients, was either ignored, treated as a sensation, or sharply criticized by those in positions of power within the professions. My statistics and theories were "wrong," I had "overstated" my case regarding the institutions of marriage and psychiatry, I'd overly "romanticized" archetypes, especially of the Goddess and Amazon variety. Moreover, I (or my book) was "strident," "hated men," and was "too angry." Like so many feminists before me, I became a "dancing dog" on the "one night stand" feminist academic and professional circuit. Luckily, I was just about to gain tenure at a university; luckily, no father, brother, or husband, wanted to psychiatrically imprison me because my ideas offended them.

It is inconceivable, outrageous, but that is *all* Elizabeth T. Stone (1842) of Massachusetts and Elizabeth Packard (1860) of Illinois did: express views that angered their brothers or husbands. Phebe B. Davis's (1865) crime was daring to think for herself in the state of New York. Davis writes: "It is now 21 years since people found out that I was crazy, and all because I could not fall in with every vulgar belief that was fashionable. I could never be led by everything and everybody." Adeline T.P. Lunt (1871) of Massachusetts notes that within the asylum, "the female patient must cease thinking or uttering any 'original expression'." She must "study the art of doffing [her] true character...until you cut yourself to [institutional] pattern, abandon hope." Spirited protest, or disobedience of any kind, would only result in more grievous punishment.

In her work on behalf of both mental patients and married women, Elizabeth Packard proposes, as her first reform, that "No person shall be regarded or treated as an Insane person, or a Monomaniac, simply for the expression of opinions, no matter how absurd these opinions may appear to others." Packard was actually trying to enforce the First Amendment on behalf of women! Packard also notes that "It is a crime against human progress to allow Reformers to be treated as Monomaniacs...if the Pioneers of truth are thus liable to lose their personal liberty...who will dare to be true to the inspirations of the divinity within them." Phebe B. Davis (1865) is more realistic. She writes that "real high souled people are but little appreciated in this world—they are never respected until they have been dead two or three hundred years."

The talented and well-connected Catharine Beecher (1855) and the feminist writer Charlotte Perkins Gilman (1886) wanted "help" for their overwhelming fatigue and depression. Beecher, after years of domestic drudgery, and

Gilman, after giving birth, found themselves domestically disabled. Gilman couldn't care for her infant daughter; Beecher could no longer sew, mend, fold, cook, clean, serve, or entertain. Beecher writes: "What [my sex] had been trained to imagine the highest earthly felicity, [domestic life], was but the beginning of care [heartaches], disappointment, and sorrow, and often led to the extremity of mental and physical suffering...there was a terrible decay of female health all over the land." Nevertheless, both women blamed themselves; neither viewed their symptoms as possibly the only way they could (unconsciously) resist or protest their traditional "feminine" work—or overwork.

Beecher and Gilman described how they *weren't* helped—or how their various psychiatric cures damaged them even further. In Gilman's words, Dr. S. Mitchell Weir ordered her to

> live as domestic a life as possible. Have your child with you all the time. (Be it remarked that if I did but dress the baby it left me shaking and crying—certainly far from a healthy companionship for her, to say nothing of the effect on me.) Lie down an hour after each meal. Have but two hours' intellectual life a day. And never touch pen, brush or pencil as long as you live.

This regime only made things worse. A desperate Gilman decided to leave her husband and infant to spend the winter with friends. Ironically, she writes, "from the moment the wheels began to turn, the train move, I felt better."

Adjustment to the "feminine" role *was* the measure of female morality, mental health, and psychiatric progress. Adeline T.P. Lunt (1871) writes that the patient must "suppress a natural characteristic flow of spirits or talk... [she must] sit in lady-like attire, pretty straight in a chair, with a book or work before [her], 'inveterate in virtue', and that this will result in being patted panegyrically on the head, and pronounced 'better'." According to Phebe B. Davis (1865),

> Most of the doctors employed in lunatic asylums do much more to aggravate the disease than they do to cure it.... It is a pity that great men [the asylum doctors] should be susceptible of flattery; for...when there is a real mind, that will flatter no one, then you will see the Doctor's revengeful feelings all out...[any] patient who will not minister to the self-love of the physicians, must expect to be treated with great severity.... Doctors have been flattered so much they are fond of admiration.

Margaret Starr (1904) of Maryland writes: "I am making an effort to win my dismissal. I am docile; I make efforts to be industrious."

How did these women of the asylum get *into* the asylum? The answer is: most often, against their will and without prior notice. Here is what happened. Suddenly, unexpectedly, a perfectly sane (or a troubled) woman would find herself being arrested by a sheriff, removed from her bed at dawn, or "legally kidnapped" on the streets, in broad daylight. Or: her father, brother, or husband might ask her to accompany him to see a friend to help him with a legal matter. Unsuspecting, the woman would find herself before a judge and/or a physician, who certified her "insane" on her husband's say-so. Often, the woman was not told she was being psychiatrically diagnosed or removed to a mental asylum. Why did this happen?

Battering, drunken husbands had their wives psychiatrically imprisoned as a way of continuing to batter them; husbands also had their wives imprisoned in order to live with or marry other women. Tirzah Shedd (1862) of Illinois writes that

> There is one married woman [here] who has been

21

imprisoned seven times by her husband, and yet she is intelligent and entirely sane.... When will married women be safe from her husband's power?

Ada Metcalf (1876) of Illinois writes:

It is a very fashionable and easy thing now to make a person out to be insane. If a man tires of his wife, and if befooled after some other woman, it is not a very difficult matter to get her in an institution of this kind. Belladonna and chloroform will give her the appearance of being crazy enough, and after the asylum doors have closed upon her, adieu to the beautiful world and all home associations.

In 1861, Susan B. Anthony and Elizabeth Cady Stanton wrote:

Could the dark secrets of those insane asylums be brought to light...we would be shocked to know the countless number of rebellious wives, sisters and daughters that are thus annually sacrificed to false customs and conventionalisms, and barbarous laws made by men for women.

Alice Bingham Russell (1898) of Minnesota was legally kidnapped by a sheriff on her husband's orders. After obtaining her own release, Russell spent twelve years trying to document and "improve the conditions of the insane." Russell describes many women whose husbands psychiatrically imprisoned them in order to gain control of their wives' property. Russell describes a woman who refused to

sell her property to suit the caprice of her husband...this young and capable woman who has been doing, up to the very hour before [she was legally kidnapped], all her housework, including the care of two children, leaves a good home and property worth $20,000.00, to become a public charity and mingle and associate continuously with maniacs.

At 32, the unmarried Adriana Brinkle (1857) of Pennsylvania conducted an economic transaction on her own: she sold some furniture she no longer needed. Charges were brought against her for selling furniture for which she had not fully paid. For the crime of embarrassing her father's view of "family honor," Brinckle's physician-father, and his judge friend, sentenced Brinckle to 28 *years* in a psychiatric hospital. Russell (1898) also tells us of a woman "who had been wronged out of some property [and who was] about to take steps to recover it when she [was] falsely accused and sent to the asylum by fraud."

Any sign of economic independence or simple human pride in a woman could be used against her, both legally and psychiatrically. Russell describes the following:

A woman and her husband quarrel; the wife with independence accepts a position as janitress, hoping her absence will prove her worth at home. She returns to secure some clothing, and learning from a neighbor that a housekeeper is in possession, and being refused admittance, she, in her haste to get justice, takes some of the washing from the clothes line, including some of the husband's and the housekeeper's to give evidence of their living together. That evening she is arrested, but has not the least fear but that she can vindicate herself. To her surprise she is without friends or counsel committed to the St. Peter asylum.

Some women of the asylum evolve rather clear-minded views on the subject of marriage and husbands. Like Catharine Beecher, Mrs. L.C. Pennell (1883) of Indiana believed something was truly "wrong" with her ("nervous prostration"), when she could no longer perform her domes-

23

tic duties. Mrs. Pennell suffered doubly when her family "charged [her] with...feigning insanity to evade the responsibilities of [her] home duties." Mrs. Pennell's husband finally had her institutionalized; but he did not visit her for nine months. Of that first visit, Mrs. Pennell writes:

> Only a moment ago I was feeling so utterly wretched and alone. But my husband had come, and he did care something for me after all. After I had entered the room, and closed the door, he stood looking at me, but not speaking a word until I said, "For heaven's sake, don't stand there staring at me in such a manner as that; sit down and say something to me... "Were you insane when you were married?" Not one single, little word of kindness or gesture of tenderness, not the shadow of a greeting, simply this cruel, calculating question. Evidently, he had even then formed the determination that I should never leave that asylum alive.... I answered "I was not insane when we were married." I have changed my opinion since then, materially, and willingly admit I was insane, and my most pronounced symptom was that I married him.

Some asylum women did not speak; some spoke and made no sense. Some wept incessantly; some were violent. However, most women in asylums did not start out—or even become—insane. According to Adeline T.P. Lunt (1871),

> A close, careful study and intimacy with these patients (finds no) irregularity, eccentricity, or idiosyncracy, either in language, deportment, or manner, than might be met with in any society of women thrown together, endeavoring to make the most of life under the most adverse and opposing circumstances.

The women of the asylum feared, correctly, that they might be driven mad by the brutality of the asylum itself, and by their lack of legal rights as women and as prisoners. As Adriana Brinckle (1857–1885) writes: "An insane asylum. A place where insanity is made." Sophie Olsen (1862) writes: "O, I was so weary, weary; I longed for some Asylum from 'Lunatic Asylums'!" According to Mrs. L.C. Pennell (1883),

> The enforcement of the rules of the institution is the surest way in the world to prevent recovery. And the brutal methods of enforcing such rules call loudly for a law which will secure to insane people the right to a chance for mental preservation.

Jane Hillyer (1919–1923) of —— notes that:

> (Asylum) conditions were so far removed from normal living that they actually aided my sense of cleavage, rather than cleared it up, as they are supposed to do. The few habits of ordinary living that remained with me were broken down by a new and rigidly enforced routine.... My last moorings were cut.

Margaret Isabel Wilson (1931) of —— says:

> We had no wholesome activities, no work and no play.... I was afraid of incarceration; I had seen too much of the deadly effects of institutionalization; and I knew that any neurotic subject might break down utterly under the strain...
>
> To sum up the effects of my asylum experiences: when I entered I had sufficient money in the bank, some real estate, chattels and personal belongings; a position, a fine constitution, and a fair chance to go on with my teaching. My money was wasted, possessions lost, and friends disappeared; I was left with bad nerves, an impaired constitution, and a weakened heart. Courage remained...I am only one of the many in Blackmoor.

Are these women of the asylum exaggerating or lying? Are they deluded? Obviously not. Each account confirms every other account. Each woman says, quite simply, that she and *every other woman she ever met in the asylum* were psychologically degraded, indentured as servants, and physically tortured by male doctors and especially by female attendants. At times, these accounts of the asylum are unbearable to read, but if the victims have documented the atrocities for us, I feel obliged to quote them at length.

[1862] Sophie Olsen:

> The faces of many [women] were frightfully blackened by blows received, partly from each other...but mostly from their [female] attendants.... I have seen the attendant strike and unmercifully beat [women] on the head, with a bunch of heavy keys, which she carried fastened by a cord around her waist: leaving their faces blackened and scarred for weeks. I have seen her twist their arms and cross them behind the back, tie them in that position, and then beat the victim till the other patients would cry out, begging her to desist...I have seen her strike them prostrate to the floor, with great violence, then beat and kick them.

[1865] Phebe B. Davis:

> There was one very interesting lady who died in one of the water closets...this closet is one of the most loathsome places imaginable; the stench was terrible...[she was] rather tall and thin, and very delicate.... She was rather a troublesome patient, and suicidal, they said. The fact is, that woman had been frightened out of her wits, and then she was literally murdered in that house, for she was worn out by brute-like treatment that I was witness to; I never saw an old canal-horse that was handled more roughly than that lady was when being harnessed down to the bedstead; the girls [attendants] did

not know that I saw that.... I thought that she could not live long, and she did not; she was a lady of very delicate sensibilities, and of course her powers of endurance were feeble.... I would advise all who take their friends to the Asylum, to cut their hair very short indeed; it is much better for the patients to have their hair cut off short than to have it pulled out by the roots...there is no prevention against the attendants making halters of the hair of patients.

[1880] Clarissa Caldwell Lathrop:

On the floor, on straw mattresses, lay poor, sick, or insane women, chained or strapped by the wrists to the floor, huddled together like sheep...the utter heartlessness of this treatment filled me with indignation and sympathy.

[1898] Alice Bingham Russell:

People are sometimes driven insane by treatment and despair in the hospital.... One woman, a Mrs. Murray, was brought to the asylum almost dying of paralysis. They made her walk the floor and beat her to make her dress herself, saying she was stubborn. I protested against such treatment and dressed the woman myself. In the morning she was dead and the doctors called it by some long name.

[1902] Margaret Starr:

I found myself [strait-jacketed] and in the room adjoining that of a blind girl.... She announced that she had been in the one room for four years; was not allowed to enter church, nor to take outdoor exercise. She was trying, she said, to save her soul and be reconciled to her imprisonment. That Madam Pike [the female attendant] kept her well dressed but doomed her to live alone....

PATRIARCHY

[1919–1921] Sally Willard:

Dr. Reginald Bolls [greeted me] with an airy gesture—the sweeping salute of a hand that touched his forehead, curved outward in a wide arc, and dropped smartly to his side. "Physically you're as sound as a bell...all we have to do is turn our attention to those foolish little foibles and fancies of yours, straighten them out, and send you back home to your good husband again...

Dr. Cozzens is a young man with beetling eyebrows and fierce black eyes and a Method. A "personal and individual method of treatment" [sic] based on a "personal and individual theory of human nature" [sic].... "Everyone's been too confounded good to you around here—that's what's wrong with you now, and it's all that's wrong, too. Everybody's given in to you, and been s-s-so sorry for you, and wept great hot salt tears over you. How about giving a thought now and then to your husband for instance? Or your father? It wouldn't hurt you any to wake up to the fact that you're doing them harm—with your 'troubles.' You've managed to make them both half sick."

[1931] Margaret Isabel Wilson:

I was like the famous elastic cat—[who] was frozen, burnt, boiled, and poured out of a bung-hole—and then the cat came back!...There was no liberty at all for us. We learned to jump up briskly at the sound of the rising bell, to dress speedily without answering back. I tried to dress as quickly as I could, for I did not wish to be called "fresh"....We could not get a bit of privacy.... Conversation during meals was taboo...

[1943–1950] Frances Farmer:

During those [eight] years, I deteriorated into a wild, frightened creature, intent only on survival.... I was raped by orderlies, gnawed on by rats, and poisoned by tainted food.... I was chained in padded cells, strapped into straight jackets, and half drowned in ice baths.... I crawled out mutilated, whimpering, and terribly alone.

But I did survive.

The three thousand and forty days I spent as an inmate inflicted wounds to my spirit that could never heal.... I learned there is no victory in survival—only grief.... Where I was, wild-eyed patients were made trustees.... Sadists ruled wards. Orderlies raped at will. So did doctors. Many women were given medical care only when abortions were performed. Some of the orderlies pimped and set up prostitution rings within the institution, smuggling men into the outbuildings and supplying them with women. There must be a twisted perversion in having an insane woman, and anything was permitted against them, for it is a common belief that "crazy people" do not know what is happening to them.

Some women of the asylum believe that their inability to function deserved a psychiatric label and a hospital stay. Two of these 27 women feel they were helped in the asylum and afterwards by a private physician. Lenore McCall (1937–1942) of —— writes that she recovered because of the insulin coma therapy. She also attributes her recovery to the presence of a nurse, who had "tremendous understanding, unflinching patience [and whose] sole concern was the good of her patient." After Jane Hillyer (1919–1923) was released from the asylum, she consulted a private doctor who she feels rescued her from ever having to return. Hillyer writes:

> I knew from the first second that I had made harbor. I dropped all responsibility at his feet.... I need not go another step alone. I perceived at once the penetrating quality of his understanding.... He said afterwards he felt as if he were the Woodsman in the fairy tale who finds

the lost Tinker's daughter in a darkly enchanted forest....
I am sure the necessity of intelligent after-care cannot be
sufficiently stressed.... My relief was indescribable. If
ever one human being went down into the farthest places
of desolation and brought back another soul, lost and
struggling, that human being was the Woodsman.

McCall and Hillyer are decidedly in the minority.
Twenty-five women of the asylum document that power is
invariably abused: that fathers, brothers, husbands, judges,
asylum doctors, and asylum attendants will do anything that
We, the People, allow them to get away with; and that wom-
en's oppression, both within the family and within state institutions, remained constant for more than a century in the
United States. (It exists today still, and in private offices as
well as in private and state institutions.)

Do these accounts of institutional brutality and torture
mean that mental illness does not exist, that women (or men)
in distress don't need "help," or that recent advances in psy-
cho-pharmacology, or insights gained from the psycho-ana-
lytic process, or from our treatment of sexual and domestic
violence victims, are invalid or useless? Not at all. What these
accounts document is that most women in asylums were not
insane; that "help" was not to be found in doctor-headed,
attendant-staffed, and state-run patriarchal institutions, either
in the nineteenth or in the twentieth centuries; that what we
call "madness" can also be caused or exacerbated by injus-
tice and cruelty, within the family, within society, and in asylums; and that personal freedom, radical legal reform, and
political struggle are enduringly crucial to individual mental
and societal moral health.

These 27 accounts are documents of courage and
integrity. The nineteenth-century women of the asylum are
morally purposeful, philosophical, often religious. Their
frame of reference, and their use of language, is romantic-

Christian and Victorian. They write like abolitionists, transcendentalists, suffragists. The twentieth-century women are keen observers of human nature and asylum abuse—but they have no universal frame of reference. They face "madness" and institutional abuse alone, without God, ideology, or each other.

What do these women of the asylum think helped them or would help others in their position? Friends, neighbors, and sons sometimes rescued the women; however, many of the nineteenth-century women obtained their freedom only because laws existed or had recently been passed that empowered men who were not their relatives to judge their cases fairly. Therefore, for them, obtaining and enforcing their legal rights was a priority. Elizabeth Packard (1860) became a well-known and effective crusader for the rights of married women and mental patients; Mrs. L.C. Pennell (1883) also suggested reforms, as did Mrs. H.C. McMullen (1894–1897) of Minnesota who, while imprisoned, wrote some model Laws for the Protection of the Insane. As noted, Alice Bingham Russell (1898) documented the stories of still-imprisoned women and helped them obtain their freedom. Mrs. Pennell (1883) for example, proposed that:

> Every doctor, after being called to examine a person for insanity shall immediately notify the proper authorities; that all persons confined in any asylum...be allowed to sleep; that the excessive habit of using opium, tobacco, or intoxicating liquors, shall disqualify any man for Superintendent, or a subordinate position in any hospital.

Mrs. McMullen proposed that

> All rules and laws for the protection of the hospital inmates should be posted up and enforced. It would be a relief of mind to know what rights they can

demand.... Those who work should be allowed com-
pensation for it.... Patients shall have the right to cor-
respond with whom they please.... Letters written by
patients shall be by them dropped into a letter box....
Friends shall be allowed to see patients.... All new
attendants should be over thirty years of age.... It is
unjust to compel elderly people to submit to the judg-
ment of the young and giddy.

In addition to legal reform, and the liberty to leave an
abusive husband or an abusive asylum, what else proved
helpful, or invaluable, to the women of the asylum? Phebe B.
Davis (1865) writes that "Kindness has been my only medi-
cine"; Kate Lee (1902) of Illinois proposes that "Houses of
Peace" be created, where women could learn a trade and save
their money, after which they could "both be allowed and
required to leave." Lee suggests that such "Houses of Peace"
"operate as a home-finder and employment bureau...thus
giving each inmate a new start in life [which] in many cases
[will] entirely remove the symptoms of insanity." Margaret
Isabel Wilson (1931) of —— says that "Nature was her doctor." Leaving the asylum helped Wilson. She writes:

> "It took me months to get over the effects of my incar-
> ceration.... Through companionship, my appetite came
> back; I could sleep in peace, and there was nobody to
> annoy me. There were no maniacal shrieks to make me
> shudder; no attendants to yell out orders; no nurses to
> give me arsenic and physics; no doctors to terrify
> me...the things [I] sorely missed while institutionalized:
> (1) liberty; (2) my vote; (3) privacy; (4) normal com-
> panionship; (5) personal letters and uncensored
> answers; (6) useful occupation; (7) play; (8) contacts
> with intelligent minds; (9) pictures, scenery, books,
> good conversation; (10) appetizing food.

I'd like Phebe B. Davis (1865) to have the last word

about why women become "excitable" and about why psychiatric hospitalization is an especially painful and outrageous form of punishment. Davis writes:

> I find that active nervous temperaments that are full of thought and intellect want full scope to dispose of their energy, for if not they will become extremely excitable. Such a mind cannot bear a tight place, and that is one great reason why women are much more excitable than men, for their minds are more active; but they must be kept in a nut-shell because they are women.

Mothers on Trial
Custody and the Baby M Case

When *Mothers on Trial: The Battle for Children and Custody* was published, the truth was out: I was not a nice, male-identified, gender-neutral liberal feminist. I was a nice woman-identified radical. I did not believe that men and women had to be the same in order to be treated equally. I mistrusted gender-neutral legislation especially in those areas where women are most obviously different from men: in the areas of reproductive biology, heterosexual and homosexual relations, pregnancy, childbirth, lactation, mother–infant bonding and the bottom-line responsibility for primary child care. After all, freedom of choice involves the right to have an abortion and the right to have and keep a baby if women so choose.

For saying all this, some feminists accused me of romanticizing the biological chains that bind us; and of biological determinism. I presumably wanted all women to be married, pregnant, and poor. I was against gender-neutral feminism and against women's right to buy or kidnap another woman's child or to rent another woman as a "surrogate uterus"—in the name of feminism.

In *Mothers on Trial* and elsewhere I note that mothers are *women* and therefore have few maternal rights and many maternal obligations; and that feminists fighting for fathers' rights or for the primacy of sperm are, to me, a pretty shabby spectacle. Were feminists in favor of joint custody because it would empower mothers (who are women) or because it would empower fathers and men, many of whom have no intention of assuming any primary child care responsibility after they win joint custody? Unfortunately, relatively few men are trying to assume *serious* child care responsibility. Even such men do not do as many things, or the same things that women do in terms of housework or children. Nor are·such men perceived in the same way as women when they perform a "female" task. However, both patriarchs and liberal feminists did not want to sacrifice joint custody as an *ideal*; many were more willing to sacrifice *real* mothers on the altar of abstract notions—real mothers who were suffering under the weight of child care responsibilities, poverty, custodial siege, and the threatened or actual loss of their children.

Once I started organizing around the Baby M case, I called many feminist leaders. For example, Betty Friedan said she was "up in arms" about what the media and the courts were doing to Mary Beth Whitehead. She said: "I am outraged by this case! Where are the feminists? Where are the feminists?"

I replied, "Well, we're a small, raggedy-assed band out there every week outside the courthouse in Hackensack. Please come and join us. But you're quite right: National NOW, New Jersey NOW, the NOW Legal Defense and Education Fund have, as yet, not gotten involved." I had this conversation with at least 30 other feminist leaders. Many were sympathetic; some became involved, but most stayed away. After a while, it became clear that the "issues" (of surrogacy, adoption, custody) were "complicated" for feminists. And why? Well, there were infertile feminists and single adoptive mother feminists and feminists who had husbands whose ex-wives really didn't deserve custody or child support. There were lesbian feminists who were suffering custodially and decent middle class feminist couples (two career families!) who couldn't adopt a child without first being humiliated. And anyway, abortion under siege was the priority.

All true. But does this mean that women should have the right to exploit other women just like men do? Or the right to call such an arrangement "feminist"?

The refusal of many feminists to get involved in the Baby M case or to agree with my view of custody did not stop them from asking me for help when one of our "own"—a custodially challenged career woman or lesbian—needed a strategy or an expert witness. But feminists still didn't see the connection between supporting Mary Beth Whitehead as a way of organizing for the reproductive and custodial rights of all women.

Custody is not a new issue for feminists. In the nineteenth century, suffragists fought in the abolitionist movement against slavery; some fought for custody for mothers. For example, there's the case of Mrs. Phelps, the wife and the sister of United States and Massachusetts state senators. When Mrs. Phelps' husband was flagrantly unfaithful, beat her, threw her down the stairs, and when she dared to complain about this—he locked her up in a mental asylum. Eventually, with her brother's help, Mrs. Phelps (whose first name I do not have) was released from this imprisonment. She ran away that very day with one of her children. Why did she have to flee with her child to retain custody? Because in the nineteenth century, and for all the previous centuries of patriarchal history, men have always owned wives and children, as legal chattel property. All during the eighteenth and nineteenth centuries, if a man divorced his wife, she was not legally entitled to ever again see her children. Like surrogate-contract mother Mary Beth Whitehead, legal wives had no legal rights.

Susan B. Anthony came to the aid of Mrs. Phelps, took

her in, helped find her sanctuary. Some of Anthony's abolitionist friends chastised her for doing so. They told her she was endangering the women's rights movement and the anti-slávery cause. Anthony disagreed. She said:

> Don't you break the law every time you help a slave to Canada? Well, the law that gives the father the sole ownership of the children is just as wicked, and I'll break it just as quickly. You would die before you would deliver a slave to his master, and I will die before I will give up the child to its father.

How many liberal, gender-neutral feminists are there today who would utter these words, who would take this risk, who would act on such a belief?

By the end of the nineteenth century, nine states and the District of Columbia finally permitted a judge—a white, middle- or upper-class male judge—to decide if a mother was wealthy enough or morally fit enough to be allowed to continue her obligation to her child. With no child support. And this was progress!

A lot has been said about how much the maternal presumption, a legal doctrine, favors mothers. Let me tell you: the maternal presumption never meant anything in a court of law when the father said, "Well, your honor, this mother has no money. She's been a go-go dancer. I think she's mentally unstable. She's narcissistic. She dyes her hair." For reasons like these, mothers have been denied not just custody but even visitation. These were some of the "deep" psychological problems that William Stern and the court used to deny Mary Beth Whitehead her parental rights (parental usually means paternal, not maternal).

Contrary to myth, when custody is *contested*, fathers win easily and routinely. It is a very different situation when the issue is child support. When a father walks out, there is

38

very little a wife can do to make him stay, make him pay decently (above the level of state welfare), or to make him see his own children. This is the common plight of most custodial mothers. Most fathers don't fight for custody. Most mothers are stuck with it, whether they want it or not. Most mothers rise to this occasion heroically, with no help from anyone. But when fathers fight for custody, fathers win custody anywhere from 60% to 82% of the time, even when they're grossly unfit, as fathers or as husbands, and even when they've never been their child's primary caretaker.

In my study, in the United States, between 1961 and 1981, 82 % of those fathers who *contested* custody won custody within two years. Eighty-seven percent had done no primary child care. One-third were wife batterers. More than one-third kidnapped their children and took them on "sprees." Nearly two-thirds of these fathers tried to seriously brainwash children against their mothers. Two-thirds refused to pay child support for the very children they claimed to love. It is not always the good guys who fight for and get custody. It is—at least two-thirds of the time—the bad guys who fight for custody.

Just when feminists began to organize for the right to abortion, and for equal pay for equal work, at that precise moment in history, men in every state legislature and in the judiciary, men running Hollywood studios and TV stations and newspapers, men who were economic losers and/or whose patriarchal kingdoms had begun to tremble as wives moved for divorce, men everywhere started to say, "Oh, you want equality? You want men's jobs? You want to leave us? Okay, bitch! We'll take your children. They were only on loan to you. It's our sperm and our dollars that matter. They were only on loan to you."

In the landmark case of Dr. Lee Salk against his wife, Kersten, Dr. Salk was granted custody—not because Kersten was unfit and not because he was an involved father, but because the judge found him to be more intellectually stimulating and richer than his legal wife who was, after all, only his womb-man or "surrogate uterus." Many people applauded this decision as a progressive and liberal decision—which indeed it was.

Then there's Mary Beth Whitehead's case. Mary Beth was a New Jersey housewife and mother who, for reasons unknown to me and, indeed, no real business of mine, signed a contract to be a surrogate mother. She was psychiatrically interviewed and, once a month for nine months, inseminated by Noel Keane's Infertility Center of New York.

Mary Beth was impregnated with the semen of William Stern. Dr. Stern forced her to undergo, against her will, but by contract, an amniocentesis test. Not only did he want a baby to whom he was genetically related; he wanted one who was genetically perfect.

Whitehead was contractually on notice that, if the baby was genetically defective, she must have an abortion. If she didn't have an abortion, then Dr. Stern would no longer be responsible for the child, legally or economically.

Mary Beth had the amniocentesis test. It made her so angry that she didn't tell the Sterns the sex of her child. And when it was time to deliver, she chose to have her legal husband, Richard, in the delivery room with her.

A woman faces all kinds of medical consequences and physical risks, including death, during pregnancy. Although the initial nonmedically facilitated contributions of the future mother and father are comparable—she contributes the egg, he contributes the sperm—the similarities stop there. She is pregnant for nine months. She carries the baby, feels it moving inside her. She goes through labor. She delivers. She begins to lactate. She breastfeeds the baby. Mary Beth did all these things. Additionally, throughout her life she was being socialized into motherhood. Motherhood is not what men are socialized into. William Stern's position was in no way identical to or even comparable with Mary Beth Whitehead's.[1]

On March 27, 1986, when she gave birth, Mary Beth saw that her new daughter looked like herself and like her other daughter, Tuesday. At that point, Mary Beth felt that she had made a terrible mistake. She could not honor the surrogacy contract. It was too inhumane. It was beyond her capacity to do so.

She called Noel Keane, the lawyer who in many ways functions like pimps and profiteers do in terms of women's sexual and reproductive capacities, and said, "I can't go through with this." And he allegedly replied, "Well, Mary Beth, okay. Take your baby home. We will find another surrogate mother for the Sterns. The worst that could happen is that they might want some visitation." And she allegedly said, "I'll give them all the visitation they want. I feel so bad. I feel so guilty."

Mary Beth went home and continued to breastfeed her daughter. On March 30, 1986, three days later, she let the anguished and arrogant Sterns have the baby. Within 24 hours, Mary Beth arrived at their door, distraught, weeping, having had no sleep. She pleaded, "I need to have the baby back. It's my baby. I can't give her up." The Sterns gave the baby back. (If they really thought she was crazy or an unfit mother, why would they have done so?) By April 12, 1986, Mary Beth allegedly informed the Sterns that she could not surrender her daughter. Mary Beth Whitehead continued to breastfeed and care for her for four and a half months.

The Sterns went to a lawyer, Gary Skoloff. And he, in turn, went to his colleague, Judge Harvey Sorkow. Now at this point in time, there had been no paternity test. The existing birth certificate said "Sara Elizabeth Whitehead." The baptismal certificate said "Sara Elizabeth Whitehead."

But Judge Sorkow ignored these facts. All that William Stern had to say to the judge was that he was the genetic father of the child (that it was his sperm) and that he was ready to economically support the consequences of his sperm—and yes, that the "surrogate" mother was mentally unstable.

The judge didn't say, "Well, let me interview this woman." He didn't say, "Let me interview this woman's lawyer." He didn't even say, "Well, let's at least have a psychiatric kangaroo court in my chambers." On the basis of hearsay alone, he issued a custody order, and then he ordered it enforced. So one day, five policemen, with guns drawn, came to Mary Beth Whitehead's home, handcuffed her, and threw her into the back seat of a police car. Only then did they actually read the birth certificate in her possession. The child's name was Sara Elizabeth Whitehead. But their order was for a "Melissa Stern." Scratching their heads, the police returned to the courthouse. And Mary Beth fled, with her baby daughter in her arms, to Florida.

William Stern responded by putting a lien on the Whitehead house. He effectively halted all the Whiteheads' cash flow. Remember, the Whiteheads were a struggling, working-class family while the Sterns were comfortably upper middle class.

Hiding in Florida, without any financial resources, Mary Beth had that famous conversation with Dr. Stern, a conversation he taped secretly, the one in which she threatened to kill herself and her child.

She said, "Bill, why have you done this to me and my family? Please take the lien off." And he replied, "It's my baby." She said, "It's *our* baby." And then she said, "Okay. What do you want me to do, kill myself? Is that what you want? Do you want me to kill the baby? Is that what you're asking for?" Frankly, if I had been in Mary Beth's place, I might have sounded crazier than she did. Any normal mother under those conditions would.

Detectives hunted Mary Beth down. The police and private detectives hired by the Sterns came time and again, and they finally took "Baby M" away. They did this after Mary Beth had been breastfeeding the child for four and a half months.

After that, Mary Beth was allowed to see her baby only two hours at a time, twice a week, in an orphanage with an armed sheriff standing guard over her. She had to travel four to six hours roundtrip for each of those two-hour visits.

Mary Beth Whitehead was put on trial by the legal system. But she was also put on trial by the media and by society. Watching coverage of her ordeal was, to me, like watching a version of the New Bedford, Massachusetts gang rape on the pool table, over and over again, day after day, where the men in the bar cheered the rapists on. You do something like that to a woman and you kill her. The victim of the New Bedford rape was driven out of town. She allegedly began to drink and take drugs. (I would too—wouldn't you?) And died in a car accident in Florida. They said it was an accident. It was the inevitable consequence of what the rapists and our woman-hating society did to her.

In Mary Beth Whitehead's case, it was not just a few bad guys who cheered her rapists on. It was the entire country.

Some patriarchs and feminists said, "We must have a right to make contracts. If a woman can change her mind about *this* contract—if it isn't enforced—we'll lose that right! And we'll lose the Equal Rights Amendment." They didn't consider that a contract that is both immoral and illegal isn't and shouldn't be enforceable. They didn't consider that businessmen make and break contracts every second, renegotiate them, buy themselves out—with only money at stake. Only a woman who, like all women, is seen as nothing but a surrogate uterus, is supposed to live up to—or be held down for—

the most punitive, most dehumanizing of contracts. No one else. Certainly no man.

Judge Sorkow ruled that the contract was enforceable and awarded the Sterns custody "in the best interests of the child." Indeed, this was just one of many contemporary custody battles between a legally married man and woman or between an adoptive couple and an impoverished birth mother. The child is usually awarded to the highest bidder. Whoever earns more money is seen as "better" for the child. How can a stay-at-home mother, like Mary Beth Whitehead, who earns no money, ever be seen as the better parent? Even when the mother has a comparatively lucrative career she is often seen as a selfish career-monster and therefore bad for the child.

Judge Sorkow ruled that the contract was not baby selling. However, if the baby were stillborn, or the mother miscarried, contractually the mother only gets $1,000. But if she delivers a perfect, whole, living baby, which she surrenders for adoption, then—and only then—is she entitled to the $10,000. Is this baby selling or not?

Judge Sorkow also rejected the idea that surrogacy contracts exploit women and create an underclass of breeders. He reached this conclusion even though, under the contract, the surrogate mother gets approximately 50 cents an hour. (Mary Beth refused the $10,000. It was put in escrow and the interest that accrued contractually went to William Stern.) Now think: who is going to be so economically desperate that she will be happy and grateful to get 50 cents per hour? It will probably be working-class women, impoverished women, and/or Third World women—whose fertility is seen as a resource to be plundered by men who want genetically perfect babies in their own spermatic image. This kind of genetic narcissism means that already living children who need to be adopted—poor, black, minority, disabled, abused, abandoned, neglected children—are not being adopted. As a society, none of us is adopting such children *before* we sign surrogacy contracts, and *before* we decide to reproduce ourselves biologically.

As a start, we planned a feminist press conference at the courthouse. And we kept going back. We demonstrated with whoever came to the courthouse to join us, with whoever called to offer their support. Local mothers of young children. Outraged mothers and fathers of grown children. I called on 200 feminists to join us. One liberal feminist expert in reproductive rights and motherhood said that she couldn't jeopardize her new-found celebrity as a neutral expert on network talk shows by joining us and appearing to "take sides." Another liberal feminist said that Mary Beth was too tarred and feathered and would only destroy what little "mainstream respectability" we had. A third liberal feminist said that Mary Beth was causing a lot of "anxiety" among lesbian co-mothers and infertile women who might themselves want the option of hiring someone just like her.

Eventually, the case was appealed to the New Jersey Supreme Court. The Court overturned Judge Sorkow's decision upholding the contract. It ruled that the contract was against public policy (in terms of baby selling and baby buying and in terms of the birth mother's right to change her mind) and could therefore not be enforced. And although it affirmed the lower court decision granting custody to the Sterns, the court nevertheless acknowledged Mary Beth Whitehead's status as the mother and awarded her visitation rights.

A partial victory at last. But New Jersey is just one state. Many courts in other states are hearing cases just like Mary Beth Whitehead's. They could rule in other ways.

Mary Beth Whitehead—the woman is brave. She went after what belongs to all of us. And we must not let her and others like her fight by themselves for our collective rights.

I call on everyone to join us at a rally tomorrow outside of Noel Keane's Infertility Center in NYC.

NOTES

1. Had Mary Beth wanted to donate the eggs and had their "harvesting" been painful, dangerous, or expensive, then in that case egg donation would not have been the same as sperm donation.

The Men's Auxiliary

Protecting the Rule of the Fathers

The male legal ownership of children is essential to patriarchy. Women are supposed to breed, bear, and/or socialize father-owned "legitimate" children within a father-absent and mother-blaming family. The fact that fathers are often absent, or abusive when present (incestuous, infanticidal, infantile), doesn't change what patriarchy is about—literally, "the rule of the fathers."

I have explored this paradox in each of my books: in *Women and Madness* in 1972 and in *Women, Money and Power* in 1976. In 1978, I did so more mythopoetically, in *About Men*. Long before Robert Bly, I saw men as father-wounded sons who therefore grow up to scapegoat women for their fathers' many failings. In *About Men* I said:

> How sad that men would base an entire civilization on the principle of paternity, upon male legal ownership of and presumed responsibility for children, and then never really get to know their sons or their daughters very well; never really participate, for whatever reason, in parenting, in daily, intimate fathering.

True rebellion against a father frightens sons terribly. Sons have just barely begun to overthrow their original parents, their mothers. So I was concerned with displacements of male–male rage and grief onto safe targets, onto weaker men, onto children, onto women.

I viewed male uterus envy as probably the major psychological force behind the patriarchal creation myths (God as a father-creator of humanity) and behind the consequent secular myths that held man as medical expert to be superior to woman as mother. (My Rx for men was not male separatist drum-beating sessions but feminist consciousness and activism.)

So I was not surprised when I first encountered fathers' rights activists in the late 1970s, claiming male maternal superiority and blaming women for fathers' failures. Eventually, I wrote about them in "*Mothers on Trial: The Battle for Children and Custody*" in 1986. The collective message presented by "fathers' rights" groups is a chilling one: that children belong to men (sperm donors, surrogate contract fathers, live-in boyfriends, legal husbands) when men want them, but not when men don't. Exactly who and what is the organized men's rights/fathers' rights movement?

It is patriarchy itself: the church, the state, and private enterprise, as it herds women into sex-typed, lesser lives; it is our own families, sacrificing our female members and defending our male members, even when they're known to have seriously wronged women and children. It is the profound and unending hostility women encounter—on street corners, on dates, at work; it is the exclusion of women from paid or well-paid jobs. The fathers' rights movement is the men's auxiliary to this larger men's movement.

The fathers' rights movement in America grew out of the male feminist movement and the antifeminist new Right. What the men's rights movement has done during the past 20 years is to repackage long-standing ideas about father-rights, sometimes in a progressive voice, other times in a reactionary one.

"Left-wing" (or feminist) fathers' rights activists claim that fathers have an equal right to children because men can mother also. They say that "Mother is a verb, not a noun" and "A man can be a better mother than a woman can."

"Right-wing" (or patriarchal) fathers' rights activists claim that children need a father-dominated family. They also claim that *God* is the "father" of all children and that He appointed earthly fathers as His children's custodians.

Both kinds of fathers' rights activists share certain perspectives and strategies. They claim that as men they are savagely "discriminated" against by lawyers, judges, and ex-wives in custody matters; that as men they are economically enslaved and controlled by greedy and parasitic ex-wives who prevent them from seeing their children. And they argue that men's parenting—whether on a "mothering" or a patriarchal fathering model—is sufficient and often superior to women's parenting.

There is no comparable movement for mothers' rights— that is, for custody, child support, alimony, marital property, increased levels of welfare, "free" legal counsel upon divorce, and so forth. But there should be because, despite men's movement cries of "unfair," it is in fact mothers' and children's interests that are routinely sacrificed on men's behalf.

The organized fathers' rights movement

1) campaigns against abortion rights, and sometimes against female birth control;

2) counsels men to kidnap children, either legally or illegally, and to default on alimony, health, and child-support payments;

3) lobbies against state-initiated actions against "deadbeat dads" and for programs that replace women's rights to a lawyer and a court hearing with mandatory mediation favoring joint legal custody;

4) lobbies the media and state legislatures to dismiss allegations that fathers commit incest (as lies fabricated by vindictive wives and manipulated children), manipulates anecdotes and social science data (e.g., about "battered husbands"), and demands—and commands—"equal time" in public and media discussions;

5) fails to lobby for health, education, and welfare—a family allowance appropriate to human needs and dignity.

As I began to work actively on behalf of women who were targets of this growing movement, I was surprised when liberal middle class feminists began to support fathers' rights—in the mistaken hope that if we allowed men even more rights than they already had they'd become more responsible and nurturant, at least to their own children; or if we counseled women to give up custody of children that they (and other women) would choose to devote themselves to feminist pursuits instead. In 1979, in *With Child: A Diary of Motherhood*, I wrote about chosen motherhood as a feminist and spiritual pursuit; however, many feminists were not interested in motherhood as an unmarried heterosexual impoverished woman's right.

Feminists have no difficulty uniting around the issue of women's reproductive rights and health. We all understand that the opposition to women's right to control our own bodies maintains men's power. But the issues of "fatherhood" and male parenting have proved to be far more complex and divisive. I have found that my pro-woman position embarrasses and threatens the kind of perfectly good liberal feminist who is not as concerned with a woman's right to choose motherhood when our right to abortion is in such jeopardy;

who ardently believes in the *ideal* of male (heterosexual) parenting and joint custody and in the reality of lesbian adoption, and the rights of the lesbian co-mother and adoptive couple over and against the rights of the lesbian biological mother or the nonlesbian, impoverished birth mother; the kind of feminist who views the right to have an abortion or to "choose" noncustodial motherhood as somehow morally and politically superior choices than the right to *retain* custody of the child you chose to have.

I grant that the issue is exceedingly complex and does not lend itself to simplistic solutions. Yet, as I see it, once feminists began fighting for equal pay and for the right to abortion, the backlash was on. If women wanted the right to leave men or take men's jobs away from them, then men, and the women who support them, would simply repossess women's children as well as women's bodies. While feminists, to our credit, may want to be "fair" to men, patriarchs are anything *but* "fair" to women.

Since I examined this new auxiliary backlash in *Mothers on Trial*, first published in 1986, more than 5,000 mothers have called or written. "I'm in your book," they say. "It's as if you know my story personally." Fathers' rights activists, both men and women, do not call or write. Instead, they picket my lectures and threaten lawsuits. In media debates, they literally shout at me, trying to drown out what I have to say. "Why don't you admit it?" they demand. "Ex-wives destroy men economically. They deprive fathers of visitation and brainwash the children against them. Fathers should have rights to alimony and child support. Joint custody should be mandatory. Why do you refuse to see it our way? We've already convinced legislators and lawyers, judges and social workers, psychiatrists and journalists—and many feminists—that what we're saying is true."

Indeed they have. I know about their convictions from

firsthand experience. I've been sued by fathers' rights activists and threatened with imprisonment; I've received my feminist share of obscene phone calls and death threats. After one particularly harrowing encounter with fathers rights activists in Canada, I found a dead animal at my door. Early in 1986, for the first time in U.S. history, the FBI convened a grand jury on an ostensibly domestic matter: to question me about the whereabouts of a runaway mother and her two "allegedly" sexually abused children. They had reason to believe I'd helped her. Friends: 1986 was not my favorite year. But in part because of the intense reaction to my work, I've come to think of myself as an abolitionist opposed to female slavery. I've learned to take myself seriously—not only because others support my views, but because they oppose them.

What is different about the face of this backlash is that some feminists support it. They argue that the best way to achieve women's liberation is through a "gender-neutral" approach—by treating women and men, mothers and fathers, as if they were the same; i.e., all white men and as such, deserving of equality. But men and women, mothers and fathers, are not equal under patriarchy. And the "gender-neutral" approach often backfires.

In *Mothers on Trial*, I challenged the myth that fit mothers always win custody—indeed, I found that when fathers fight they win custody 70 % of the time, even when they have been absentee or violent fathers. Since then, other studies have demonstrated that when men fight they win custody anywhere from 50% to 80% percent of the time—whether or not they have been involved in child care or the economic support of the family.

Although 80% to 85% of custodial parents are mothers, fathers who *fight* win custody not because mothers are unfit or because fathers have performed any housework or child care, but because mothers are held to a much higher standard of parenting.

In custody battles, mothers are routinely punished for having a career or job (she's a "selfish absentee mother") *or* for staying home on welfare (she's a "lazy parasite"); for committing heterosexual adultery or for living with a man out of wedlock (she's "setting an immoral example") *or* for remarrying (she's trying to "erase the real dad") or for failing to provide a male role model (she's a "bitter, man-hating lesbian").

Divorcing fathers increasingly use the threat of a custody battle as an economic bargaining chip. And it works. He gets the house, the car, and the boat; she gets the kids and, if she's lucky, minimal child support. When fathers persist, a high percentage win custody because judges tend to view the higher male income and the father-dominated family as in the "best interests of the child." Many judges also assume that the father who fights for custody is rare and should therefore be rewarded for loving his children, or that something is wrong with the mother.

What may be "wrong" with the mother is that she and her children are being systematically impoverished, psychologically and legally harassed, and physically battered by the very father who is fighting for custody. However, mothers are often custodially punished for leaving a violent husband (she's "economically depriving her kids and violating her marriage vows") *or* for staying (she "married him so I hold her responsible for what he did"). Some people, including psychiatrists, lawyers, and judges, deal with male domestic violence by concluding that women have either provoked or exaggerated it.

Co-parenting or "male mothering" is an ideal of some feminist theorists, who therefore support joint custody of children as the preferred arrangement after divorce. However, this is liberal theoretics, not scientific fact—and leaders of the joint custody movement such as Dr. Judith Wallerstein are now saying just this. Inviting men to have more involvement in childcare, through a joint custody arrangement, will not necessarily produce more "mothering," but perhaps more patriarchal "fathering." The "disconnected" men who have been socialized to reproduce sexism are the very men whom feminists have been calling upon to participate "equally" in child care. Dr. Miriam Johnson, in *Strong Mothers, Weak Wives*, concludes that fathers—not mothers—control and dominate gender stereotyping. She asks: Would not such men "carry their dominating tendencies" into the nursery? Do we really want such men involved in mothering?

I am absolutely in favor of getting men off the battle-fields and into the kitchen; and absolutely in favor of male tenderness, intimacy, accountability. However, I am arguing that the call for "gender neutrality" in custodial determination is a mistake. A deeper and closer look at the way "gender neutrality" works in actual custody cases shows that, rather than achieving equality, it may enhance male, patriarchal power and the primacy of sperm.

The patriarchal ideal of fatherhood is sacred. As such, it usually protects each father from the consequences of his actions. The ideal of motherhood is sacred, too, but no human mother can live up to it, so it serves to expose all mothers as imperfect. Therefore, *all* mothers are custodially vulnerable because they are women; *all* fathers, including incestuous, violent, absent, passive, or "helper" fathers, can win custody, not because mothers are "unfit" or because fathers are truly equal partners, but because fathers are men.

The equal treatment of "unequals" is unjust. In real patriarchy, the paternal demand for "equal" custodial rights, and the law that values legal paternity or male economic superiority over biological motherhood and/or over women's primary care of children, degrades and violates both mothers and children.

A Wolf in
Feminist Clothing

These are the times that try feminist souls. "Femininity's" back—even among feminists—and for years, I'd thought it was a fugue state, not a secret political weapon. It's 1994 and we're still surrounded by ancien regime images of glamorous, mainly white, young, thin, lucky-in-love, rich women, who by media sleight-of-hand, have become our radical feminist "leaders." I despair when mediocrity triumphs —when people confuse what sells with what's important or true.

I find the current crop of books for women disturbingly slick, and deeply reactionary. Yes, Camille Paglia, Katie Roiphe (*The Morning After*), Marianne Williamson (*A Woman's Worth*) and Naomi Wolf (*Fire With Fire*), are frequently quoted, not because they're original or revolutionary thinkers, but because what they say threatens no one—at least, no one in power and no wannabes. The media-anointed "leaders" insist that:

- Anita Hill prevailed (even though Clarence Thomas is a sitting Supreme Court Justice).

- There is no epidemic of rape and incest (only an epidemic of malicious, feminist-induced hysteria, false memory syndrome, and fake statistics about rape, gang-rape, and date-rape).

- Women have won the gender war—even as women from Paris to Peoria are overworked, unpaid, underpaid, devalued, undervalued—and yes, "glass-ceilinged"; even as women are being gang-raped in Bosnia and Boston, genitally mutilated in Mogadishu and Nairobi, killed at birth in Beijing and Calcutta, sold into sexual slavery as children in Bangkok and Manila, and veiled, beheaded, and stoned to death for "adultery" in Saudi Arabia and in the Iranian provinces.

Women have not won the war against women; we have only begun to fight. The heat of battle is intense. Many women are running scared, smiling as fast as they can. Clearly, it's too hot in the kitchen for Naomi Wolf and she's made her exit; that she insists on describing her departure as "*radical* feminism" is sheer Newspeak. While Wolf's first book, *The Beauty Myth*, exposed how media images of "perfection" were harmful to women, *Fire With Fire* seems to be written *for* the media—as if Wolf's applying for a job as a news anchor or syndicated columnist. No crime, by the way, but no book either.

Vital feminist ideas are rarely, not frequently, touted in the mainstream media; it's important to understand what's being shown as the latest in radical feminist "fashion," as worn by a well-spoken, exceedingly earnest, and personable young woman.

Wolf proclaims a "genderquake"—then, paradoxically, backtracks, as she tries to explain why, in her view, so many women have resisted the feminist label. She describes some of the feminist sisterhood accurately, but constantly cuts her own insights down to size in a voice that is shockingly similar to women's magazine advice.

A Wolf in Feminist Clothing

Wolf's message, to women only, is: Improve yourself, your self-esteem, your appearance, your attitude—and pay no attention to the high female body count. Don't analyze it or draw political conclusions. All is sunny, couldn't be better. No pain, all gain.

Wolf describes the feminist sisterhood at its worst—and she's accurate about the collective authoritarianism, the "horizontal hostility," the downward mobility, the worm's eye view of realpolitik. But you can find precisely such self- and woman-hating behavior among women everywhere: in church groups, sororities, and families. Proclaiming oneself a "feminist" doesn't, unfortunately, inoculate one from sexist behaviors.

However, Wolf is wrong about some important things. For example, the pioneering shelter workers didn't refuse money for their volunteer labor; no one offered any. Taking token sums of government money meant the files were open to Reagan-Bush government surveillance and that the female victims of violence would be forced into therapy, not into political activism. If a battered mother was running away with her sexually abused children the therapist would be forced to "tell" on her. Shelter workers were, understandably, ambivalent about accepting token sums of money under such conditions.

Wolf's experience in a rape crisis center was with her third-wave peers, not with their pioneering mothers. Their style may partly have been an imitation of second-wave feminist culture—and partly more of the same *non-feminist* female behavior that Wolf abhors ("backstabbing," denying one's own "dark" side, rewarding the weakest, punishing the strongest, ruling by excluding, taking no prisoners). Join any ladies' auxiliary and you'll experience these same dynamics.

Wolf's redefinition of radical feminism includes: 1) a "go along, get along" approach to power; 2) the idea that feminism doesn't need principles—sound-bites, such as "I feel your pain, I see your point" will do; and 3) the recommendation that women should stop concentrating on "victimization" and seize the "power" that is ours.

According to Wolf, one reason that some women shy away from calling themselves feminists is that others might suspect them of being lesbians. "Not all women can economically afford to be seen as gay—and if they are not gay, the misidentification is a financial, emotional, and physical risk few are willing to run," writes Wolf. Ah, risk. What if the Danes had chosen not to wear Yellow Stars because it was too dangerous, and because they weren't Jews anyway? The Jews of Denmark might all have died in Auschwitz.

Wolf describes herself as a practitioner of "radical heterosexual feminism." She writes: "Male sexual attention is the sun in which I bloom. The male body is ground and shelter to me, my lifelong destination. When it is maligned categorically, I feel as if my homeland is maligned." Is she not "of woman born"? I thought that "our bodies, ourselves," our *own* female bodies were the sovereign territory feminists wanted. She also contradicts herself: one page later, she writes that "there is a primal place that leads plumb down to infancy...she [the infant] wants to possess the breast...she wants to merge, be cared for, taken over." Is the female breast not "homeland" to women as well as men? Even that Victorian gentleman, Dr. Freud, conceded we were probably all "bisexual."

Radical heterosexuality? Okay, I'm open. Persuade me that who I sleep with, or my declaration that I can't do without sexual pleasure, is somehow equivalent to a political analysis, or to a program that will abolish rape or establish economic equality for women and for all races and classes.

I didn't think Gennifer Flowers mattered; I was more interested in Bill Clinton's voting record on women. I am more concerned with our leaders' out-of-bed than their in-bed positions. Given how overexposed and overly controlled women are as physical/sexual beings, I don't want to know too much about the personal or sexual life of Janet Reno, Barbara Mikulski, Ruth Bader Ginsburg, Donna Shalala, or Hillary Clinton (though I agree with Wolf: I would be concerned if they, or any public official or employer, sexually harassed their employees).

I don't mind heterosexual Femme glitter. Sher Hite, Germaine Greer, Gloria Steinem, Joan Nestle, and many others were always very good at it, still are. It's okay, as long as you also have politics and a real sense of humor about surface appearances. (Steinem has said she's "not really that pretty, the media just thinks [she's] pretty *for a feminist.*")

I've always preferred Maria Callas to Jackie Onassis—nothing personal, I just don't like the less-is-more school of female appeal. I prefer the fleshy to the anorexic, the greatly to the minimally talented. I worry when men (and women) reward women merely for being younger, for knowing less, and for saying things that are less rather than more threatening.

I have no problem with a woman of ideas declaring that she is a sexual being. It's important for a thinking, feminist woman to tell her straight, lesbian, bisexual, and celibate sisters that her body is her own (see my above point about our bodies, ourselves), and that she won't lie with her body to toe a party line. But it's as important—no, it's more important—to deliver the same message to powerful anti-lesbian and anti-homosexual groups. It's called "talking truth to power" and the young are often gifted at this. Not Wolf, not Roiphe, not Williamson, who are telling men just what they want to hear: that modern women, even those with feminist longings, still burn for male sexual attention, approval, and protection, exclusively. So young, and such canny gate-keepers already.

Wolf ends her book with a series of Psychological

Strategies. Her first five admonish us to

> 1) avoid generalizations about men that imply that their maleness is the unchangeable source of the problem; 2) avoid generalizations about men that are totalizing: that is, that do not admit to exceptions; 3) never choose to widen the rift between the sexes when the option exists to narrow it, without censoring the truth; 4) never unreflectingly judge men in a way that we would consider sexist if men applied it to women...; 5) distinguish between the men we love, who are on our side, and the male system of power, which we must resist. It is not "hating men" to fight sexism. But the fight against sexism must not lead to hating men...

Contrast this tone with her otherwise matter-of-fact (and quite useful) description of the difficult "impasse" often faced by African-American and white women trying to work together. Wolf demands more of women than she does of men.

> To antiracist white women, the impasse is a devastating rejection, like a lover's. "Aren't we listening?" they ask. "Aren't we trying to address the issues?" To African-American women, that very articulation of the problem is often annoying, for it sounds as if white women believe that their good intentions will make racism disappear overnight, at which point everything will be fine. White women's wish for intimacy and love from African-American women often carries the implicit hope of being magically absolved of racism... If we learned to substitute respect for intimacy and teamwork for sisterhood, these tensions would not paralyze women's organizational efforts...

Wolf shows us African-American and white women working on racism together; she does not show us women and men working on sexism together. We don't read: "It sounds as if men believe that their good intentions will make sexism disappear overnight." Instead, Wolf shows us men and women "loving" each other and having "sex" together.

I'm all in favor of alliances with pro-woman or feminist men in the boardroom, in the bedroom, and on the barricades. But I think it's cowardly, and insulting, to appeal to men by saying that feminists *personally* love and adore men—all men, any men—and/or that feminism doesn't really threaten the status quo because feminist leaders love/adore their sons, fathers, brothers, husbands, or boyfriends.

Wolf exaggerates the extent to which feminists have offended or destroyed "good men." (*Fire With Fire* might well be called *Women Who Don't Love Good Men Enough and What's Wrong with Them*.) In her book, pro-feminist men are "nearly dismembered" when they attend radical feminist speeches. But where are the bloody body parts? Real body parts litter the landscape but they're mainly female body parts. Men have killed and dismembered them. Wolf wants to "heal this sexual divide" and to "ease rage between the sexes." That's nice, but how? As Churchill knew, appeasement doesn't work. And that's all most women have tried—that, and looking away, blaming the victim, and denying that things are "that bad."

It's disheartening to see a media-obsessed generation of young women who are more conservative than their mothers and grandmothers. Perhaps to them, the (male) power structure is background; in the foreground is the tyranny of their mothers' (or of older women's) radical feminism. Perhaps Roiphe and Wolf are engaged in a daughters' rebellion. Wolf is consistently ambivalent about both radical and liberal second-wave feminists, especially those who have paid a high price for their political beliefs; I believe Wolf and others of her generation fear this deeply.

According to Wolf, some women have remained alienated from feminism either because the media has distorted the essentially happy-go-lucky nature of revolutionaries or because those same revolutionaries have, wrongfully, insisted on certain principles or "dogmas." Abortion rights, for example. Or so-called generalizations about male aggression.

Wolf writes: "I am calling on us to look clearly at the epidemic of crimes against women without building a too-schematic world view upon it." But just mopping up after the violence that has been done to woman after woman after woman is not as effective as "schematically" confronting that same violence. Physicians used to treat brown lung disease in miner after miner; unionists eventually went out on strike to close mines down and to improve working conditions.

How, exactly, shall women (and men of good will) go out on strike to end rape? Wolf, Roiphe, Paglia, and Williamson do not join Andrea Dworkin in calling for even a "24-hour truce"—no rape for 24 hours. Instead, Roiphe insists that reports of date rape are greatly exaggerated. Wolf suggests that we decorate rape crisis shelters in a more cheerful fashion. She may have a point, but it's beside the point. Rape centers aren't starving "for lack of fun," but for lack of available funds, lack of political action. Or is rape something Wolf, as a radical feminist, is willing to live with?

What's Wolf's program? She has one. She demands that we not discriminate against anyone on the basis of gender; she insists, correctly, that this is a radical goal. I agree with her. But this is a hard goal to reach, especially if we don't note our starting point. Currently, both women and men discriminate against men *positively*—we adore, trust, fear, and forgive men; we despise, mistrust, fear, and punish women—we discriminate against women *negatively*. Reaching some middle ground is a laudable aim. Wolf doesn't take us there. What she does, instead, is to passionately defend the "good" men—whom she perceives as under massive and unfair feminist attack—and attack the "bad" women, mainly second-wave feminists, now in their 50s and 60s (I'm one) whom she blames/jettisons first for not having attracted a mass following and/or for having poor image control: as if popularity and "image" are all that count, as if her so-called "genderquake" wasn't brought about by 28 years of hard, second-wave feminist labor.

Wolf takes a cheap shot when she opposes "victim" to "power" feminism. By all means, let's not be victims, let's have power feminism. But Wolf fakes power like some women fake orgasm.

She criticizes the so-called "victim feminists" for attempting to deal with violence against women in a political way. From about 1967 on, in addition to fighting for women's right to abortion and to equal pay for equal work, grass-roots feminists focused on the sexual objectification of women and on issues of sexual violence toward women, such as stranger-rape and sexual harassment on the job and on the street. They pioneered and maintained the rape crisis centers and the shelters for battered women, conducted Speakouts, testified at hearings, and drafted legislation. Only after a decade were feminist activists able to expand their focus to include marital rape, date rape, domestic battery, and incest.

During the 1980s, it became clear to feminists working in the area that most prostituted women were also incest victims, that many battered wives were treated as if they were their husband's or boyfriend's prostitutes, that wife-batterers, pedophiles, and serial killers of women often admit they're addicted to pornography, and that all women, whether they were prostitutes (the so-called "bad girls") or non-prostitutes (the so-called "good girls"), who dared to kill in self-defense were treated as if they were prostitutes, i.e. demon terrorists from hell who deserved no mercy.

I understand Wolf's desire to "look away"; most have.

But as the poet Judy Grahn wrote:

> Have you ever committed any indecent acts with women? Yes, many. I am guilty of allowing suicidal women to die before my eyes or under my hands because I thought I could do nothing.

A radical feminist vision has to be radical. If you're a radical, the things you say and do are bound to threaten those in power, as well as those who are at their mercy. They burned the nineteenth- and twentieth-century meeting houses down to intimidate abolitionists and suffragists into silence, and they jailed and force-fed them too.

Fighting fire with fire is brutal, bloody, deadly, dull, terrifying, unsafe, and unglamorous. Like birth. And revolution. And creation. Wolf refers briefly, very briefly, to Harriet Tubman's nineteenth-century Underground Railway: "she [Tubman] took the liberation of African-American slaves into her own hands." However, breaking the law or creating an underground is not on Wolf's menu of options when she tells her readers to exercise their right to vote, run for office, amass capital, tithe themselves, network, etc.

Recently in Brooklyn, where I live, a 20-year-old Black street-prostituted woman was gang-raped by *seven* Black teenage boys who, afterwards, laughing, doused her genitals and buttocks with gasoline and set her afire. She bolted the hospital when personnel demeaned her as a "whore." Her mother threw her out of their project apartment for "shaming" her. Now, she walks the streets, still selling (she has a pimp/manager), getting crazier and crazier, suffering horribly. Where is "North" for this poor wretch? It doesn't exist yet. Real power feminism will be needed to create it.

Does Wolf really believe that her within-the-system recipe, "Add women and stir," amounts to that real power? I agree, by all means, let's get women or *feminists*, both women and men, elected to government. But whom will we elect—and to do what, and at whose expense? Will our electioneering mainly benefit the wives, daughters, mistresses, and homosexual lovers of (white) men of wealth —or will it alleviate the suffering of the most vulnerable and endangered amongst us—now, not a century from now?

Radical thinkers pay a high price. They learn to take themselves seriously, not only because others support their views, but because others oppose them. One learns that one has power not from one's admirers or supporters, but from one's opposition. If there is no opposition, something's wrong.

I agree with Wolf: "It is not dissent that is harmful to feminism but consensus." Feminists must be able to disagree in public, take nothing personally, and keep on working together. I think Wolf has given us an opportunity to discuss what feminism is—and what it might be.

I challenge Wolf and others of her generation, and of my own, to use their moment in history to provide sanctuary in their lifetime to the victims of patriarchal violence, and to create a powerful feminist government by all the means at their disposal.

The question Wolf asks herself is: Will she choose to be a "warrior for justice" or succumb to her need to "connect and be loved"? She experiences the tension between these two desires as a "coat of fire." But women as a group are punished whether, as individuals, we acquiesce or resist. Thus, heroism—not martyrdom—is our only feminist alternative.

Feminism and Illness

In only 25 years, a visionary feminism has managed to seriously challenge, if not transform, world consciousness. Nevertheless, I am saddened and sobered by the realization that no more than a handful of feminists have been liberated from the lives of grinding poverty, illness, overwork, and endless worry that continue to afflict most women and men in America.

I have seen the best minds of my feminist generation go "mad" with battle fatigue, get sick, give up, disappear, kill themselves, die, often alone, and in terrible isolation, as if we were already invisible: to each other, and to ourselves, our role as pioneers and immigrants diminished, forgotten.

Immigrants always form infrastructure or self-help groups and tithe themselves accordingly. We are the immigrants who, in the late 1960s and early 1970s, left the Old Patriarchal Country to clear a path in History for the generations to come. It's too late for us to turn back, and we've still got "miles to go before we sleep" in our own feminist country.

There are few feminist networks in place whose mandate it is to assist feminists (or female adults) when they lose their jobs, fall ill, *stay* ill, face death, and are without patriarchal family resources, supportive mates, or other safety nets.

Surrounded by epidemics, I ask: Where are our feminist credit unions and emergency funds (remember those failed attempts in the mid-70s?)? Our feminist soup kitchens, Meals on Wheels, land trusts, and old age homes (remember those fiascos?)? Our breast cancer fundraising campaigns, our hospices, our burial societies? (Feminists are just *starting* to get serious about breast cancer, and about women with AIDS.)

They do not yet exist. Instead, feminists say: "I didn't tell anyone I was sick because I didn't want my employers or my enemies to know." Or: "I didn't ask anyone for help. Pride maybe, but also fear. People tend to avoid you when you're in trouble." One survivor of breast cancer told me that in the mid-80s, her newly formed cancer support group disbanded(!) when its first member died. A formerly disabled lesbian feminist said: "Sick men know how to get others to take care of them. Sick women don't know how to ask for help and can't get it when they do. Maybe gay men are also learning how to take care of others. Gay men took care of me when I was sick, not other lesbian feminists." A chronically disabled woman said: "Only a few friends visited me more than once. Most had a hard time with the fact that a strong woman could become so sick, and an even harder time fitting me into schedules already overcrowded with other care-taking responsibilities."[1]

Some feminists blame those whose immune systems cannot absorb any more environmental toxins—or toxic amounts of hostility. Some of us still say: "It's her own fault she has no health insurance,[2] no nursing care, no job, no mate. She should have planned better or compromised harder." Or we say: "But isn't she really a little (or a lot) crazy?"

In 1982, Elizabeth Fisher, founder of *Aphra* magazine and author of *Women's Creation: Sexual Evolution and the Shaping of Society*, and in 1987, my dear friend Ellen Franfurt, author of *Vaginal Politics*, killed themselves. Not just because they were depressed, on drugs, discarded at midlife, or without hope that things would get better (although some of this was so), but *also* because they were tired of fighting so hard for so long for a place in the sun (a community, a decent-enough book contract), tired of being hated so much and of never having enough money. They despaired of both man's and woman's inhumanity to woman.

So many of us have died, mainly of breast cancer and metastasized breast cancer. To name only a few: June Arnold, Park Bowman, Phyllis Birkby, Jane Chambers, Barbara Deming, Audre Lourde, Mary-Helen Mautner, Barbara Myerhoff, Lil Moed, Pat Parker, Barbara Rosenblum, Isacca Siegel, Sunny Wainwright.

We have no quilt, and no memorial.

So many of us have wrestled with and survived breast cancer. So many of us are struggling with long-time disabilities, reeling from Lyme Disease, and from Chronic Fatigue Immune Dysfunction Syndrome (CFIDS), myself included.[3]

Some of us have been blessed by feminist care-taking. I think of how magnificently Sandra Butler cared for—and orchestrated community support for—her cancer-stricken lover/partner Barbara Rosenblum (an account is contained in their book *Cancer in Two Voices*); I think of how tenderly, how enduringly, Jesse Lemisch has cared for his CFIDS-racked wife, my beloved comrade Naomi Weisstein; I think of how many lesbian-feminists cared for and sent "white light" to Barbara Deming and Jane Chambers, and who continue to do so for Audre Lorde.[4]

But these are splendid exceptions, lucky, individual solutions, even trends, not yet sturdy, immigrant infrastructure.

I recently attended a rent party for Ti-Grace Atkinson, author of *Amazon Odyssey*. Ti-Grace's health was seriously impaired by exposure to low dose radiation. (Her father was the head of the Atomic Energy Commission's Plutonium By-Products Division at Washington State's Hanford Reservation.) She says: "First, I had a hysterectomy. Now, I have no thyroid left. I take tons of thyroid medication, some of which has made me sick and unable to work."

The rent party was a determined, even inspired, grass-roots effort that yielded more good will than cash; however, such events are too labor-intensive, too hard to repeat on a monthly basis for every pioneer feminist, whether or not she's written a book, who's in an illness-related economic crisis.

Ti-Grace at least has an apartment. Other feminist pioneers are—or are about to become—homeless.

For example, a legendary anti-pornography activist has been forced to warehouse her files and move in with a friend. The co-author of a lesbian-feminist classic, a well-known feminist comedienne, an abortion rights activist—and countless other pioneers all sway unsteadily on the brink of joblessness and homelessness. The co-author of a much-loved book on feminist spirituality became homeless last year; she left New York for a warmer climate to be homeless in. Shulamith Firestone, author of *The Dialectics of Sex* and a welfare recipient, had to battle, hard, to hang onto her rent-controlled apartment in between "visits" to Belleview in the late 1980s.

The fact that none of these women have written second books impoverishes us all.

Two of my dear friends, both major feminist leaders, have kept writing, despite a variety of health problems, but like so many great writers, both dead and alive, simply cannot earn a living by the pen. (A writer's annual income is about $5,000.00.) Neither are independently wealthy, have tenured positions or pensions; they remain dreadfully, bravely poor, unable to act on their own grand visions without unimaginable personal sacrifice and constant worry.

I am not blaming any of us for not having done more; we did the best we could, and we did alot. But in all our imaginings, we failed to imagine that we ourselves would grow weary or fall ill and have no real, specific "family" to take us in and tide us over until we could get back on our feet.

Some of us acted as if we didn't think we'd *need* families again. Perhaps our collective experience of transcendence blinded us to our ordinary needs. But most of us were longing for "communitas." We talked about sisterhood and community, tribes and alternate families—but only in the abstract, as we rushed from one dazzling spectacle to another.

I know: the republic ought to provide employment, health insurance, and medical care for all its citizens, but it doesn't; and we have fallen on hard times, along with everyone else. All we have is each other: our sisters, ourselves.

NOTES

1. Some women either opposed or were so uncomfortable with my identifying them by name that I chose not to do so.

2. In May of 1992, the Older Women's League released a report that showed that due to low-paying and part-time work, American women between the ages of 40 and 60 are far more likely than their male contemporaries to lack health insurance.

3. Some survivors of breast cancer and other serious diseases are: Blanche Wiesen Cook, Jan Crawford, Edith Konecky, Phyllis Kriegel, Eleanor Pam, Alma Rautsong (Isabel Miller), Gloria Steinem—these names come immediately to mind. Some survivors of long-time disabilities are: Flo Kennedy, Bea Kreloff, Bettye Lane, Judy O'Neil, Betty Powell; of Lyme disease: Beverly Lowy, Max Dashu; of CFIDS: myself, Susan Griffen, Joan Nestle, Aviva Rahmani, Arlene Raven, Naomi Weisstein—to name only those I know personally.

4. Since this article first appeared, more feminists have developed breast cancer and some have died from it. I have added/changed some names accordingly.

Marcia Rimland's Deadly Dilemma

For more than 5,000 years, no mother anywhere has ever been legally and automatically entitled to custody of her own child. Only men have been *entitled* to sole custody of children. Women have been *obliged* to bear and rear children—who carry their father's last name, without which they are considered illegitimate.

Although most custodial parents in North America and everywhere else are mothers, this does not mean that women always "win" custody; rather, mothers retain custody only when fathers choose not to fight for it. In 62 countries surveyed world-wide, fathers were legally and automatically entitled to custody if they wanted custody—whether or not they fulfilled their paternal obligations.

Mothers were obligated to care for and support their children without any reciprocal rights; most rose to the occasion heroically. Nevertheless, women had few rights as *individuals* and no rights as mothers over and against the rights that men have over women, that husbands have over wives, that fathers have over mothers, and that states have over citizens. In general, mothers everywhere are vulnerable to legalized father right—whether that right is embodied by a legal or genetic father, paternal family or tribe, or by the state, acting as a surrogate father.

In the last 15 to 20 years, when American fathers fought for custody they increasingly won custody, from 63% to 70%

of the time, whether or not they were previously absent, distant, parentally non-involved, or violent (Chesler, 1986; Pascowicz, 1982; Polikiff, 1982, 1983; Takas, 1987; Weitzman, 1985). Similar trends have been documented in Canada (Lahey, 1989) and in Australia, France, Holland, Great Britain, Ireland, Norway, and Sweden (Chesler, 1991; Smart and Sevenhuijsen, 1989). Fathers do not win because mothers are unfit, or because fathers have been participatory parents, but because mothers are expected to meet more stringent standards of parenting. This double standard has also been documented by ten 1989–90 U.S. State Supreme Court reports on "Gender Bias in the Courts" which confirm that there is one set of expectations for mothers and another less demanding set for fathers.

Today more and more mothers, as well as the leadership of the shelter movement for battered women, are realizing that women risk losing custody if they seek more (or sometimes any) child support or stability from fathers in terms of visitation. Incredibly, mothers also risk losing custody if they accuse fathers of beating or sexually abusing them or their children—*even or especially if these allegations are detailed and supported by experts.*

Many judges still believe that "just because a man beats his wife doesn't mean he's an unfit father." While it is true that many children of violent fathers reject violence when they grow up, many do not. Both studies and common sense suggest that a violent, woman-hating father teaches his son to become—and his daughter to marry—a man like himself. Which, despite what some judges say, is not in the best interest of women, children, or society.[1]

What about a father who sexually molests his own child? Surely all of us, judges included, take that seriously—don't we? Not necessarily. On the one hand, we vaguely know that 16% of all young American girls (an epidemic number), and a much lower percentage of young American boys, have been sexually molested within the heterosexual family by fathers, grandfathers, uncles, stepfathers, and brothers. Yet when mothers accuse men of sexually abusing children in their families, we don't believe that they're telling the truth.

We don't, of course, *want* to believe it, but studies document that at least two-thirds of the recent maternal allegations about incest are true, not false, and that neither mothers nor child advocates allege paternal incest more often during a custody battle than at other times. Some fathers' rights activists, including lawyers and mental health experts, keep insisting that the *mothers* or children are lying or misguided. And the media continue to cite an increase in "false" maternal allegations.

A Washington, D.C. physician, Dr. Elizabeth Morgan, was jailed for more than two years for hiding her daughter, Hilary, from what she and many experts believed was an incestuous relationship with Hilary's father. The father has consistently denied any wrongdoing and was never found by any court to have sexually abused his daughter Hilary. Hilarys' theraspists were convinced that she had been sexually abused and was becoming actively suicidal. However, a Virginia judge did prevent him from seeing Hilary's half-sister Heather, from a previous marriage, who had also accused him of sexually molesting her. Judge Dixon refused to consider this as relevant to the Morgan case.

Dr. Morgan's lengthy imprisonment haunted me. Judge Herbert Dixon had made Dr. Morgan an example of what can happen to any mother who defies the law—even to save her own child.

Here's what I have to say about the Morgan case: Look what can happen to a white, God-fearing, Christian, heterosexual mother who is a physician, whose brother is a Justice

Department lawyer, whose fiancé (now husband) is a judge, and whose lawyer is an ex-State Attorney General; look what can happen to an extremely privileged "insider" who decides to make a court case of it. Morgan is an insider in terms of class, color, sexual preference, etc. As a woman, she's still an outsider. Would a *male* physician be allowed to sit in jail so long without the old boy network springing into action? Dr. Morgan was freed only by the passage of a special bill approved by Congress and the Senate and signed into law by the President. It states that in the future no judge can imprison a resident of Washington, D.C. for more than 12 months without a trial by jury for specific, stated crimes.

What if Dr. Morgan were a Black, Asian or native-Indian woman with only a high school education? A lesbian and an atheist without a single friend or relative in high places? What if the media thought the case not worth the coverage? Interestingly enough, many of the media and psychiatric reports on Dr. Elizabeth Morgan bore an uncanny resemblance to those of another mother-kidnapper: Mary Beth Whitehead. Both mothers were often described as narcissistic, righteous, stubborn, manipulative, and obsessed "borderline personalities." This is not surprising. Despite differences in class and education, both were viewed by experts who share the same biased views of women.

There is a danger in focusing exclusively on the incest-custody kidnapping battles. If we finally convince judges that some fathers do sexually abuse their children and that it's a bad thing to do, then judges might begin to deny custody to *incestuous* fathers but they'll tend to view all *non-incestuous* fathers as automatically worthy of custody—if only by comparison. Still, how can we not focus on some blatant miscarriages of justice?

Marcia Rimland was a woman driven to the edge—and over the edge—by a court system bent on thwarting her ability to protect her four-year-old daughter from harm. When I joined a demonstration called by the Coalition for Family Justice last summer to mourn the deaths of Rimland and her daughter, I was filled with both grief and rage.

It was a childcare worker and Rimland herself who first suspected that Rimland's estranged husband, Ari Adler, was sexually abusing their daughter, Abigail. Abigail began having tantrums, weeping uncontrollably, and masturbating excessively after visits to her father. After four play-and-talk sessions with Abigail, a clinical social worker validated the child's probable sexual abuse. But in Rockland County, N.Y. Family Court, the social worker's findings were challenged. Another sex abuse validator concluded there were problems with the social worker's findings, including failure to adequately explore the possibility that the child was coached by her mother. However, the second validator never evaluated the child in person.

After this report, Judge William P. Warren decided to reinstate Adler's overnight, unsupervised visits with Abigail. Marcia Rimland made a hasty appeal to the Appellate Division in Brooklyn, where a stay of Warren's order was issued—one that allowed supervised visitation by the father in the home of his friends—the very place at which the alleged sexual abuse had continually taken place. Abigail was scheduled to spend three overnight visits and a full weekend with her father before any court would reconsider the issue.

The night before the first mandated visitation, Rimland gave Abigail a tranquilizer. She and the child then sat in a red Toyota with the motor running in an enclosed garage until they both were dead from carbon monoxide inhalation. "I have no choice, I hope you understand," read Rimland's suicide note.

Many people will say that the murder-suicide proves that Marcia Rimland was crazy all along. But I believe that we should also view Rimland as a woman driven crazy—driven to despair and desperation. Although her action was personal, not political, we can analyze it politically and try to understand its meaning.

Most research shows us that when mothers or daycare workers allege paternal sexual abuse, it is very likely true. Sometimes, however, one cannot substantiate it fully or clearly enough. This does not mean that the mother has lied or that she is crazy or malevolent. It means that our techniques of eliciting information from children are not advanced enough.

Yet, in the course of writing *Mothers on Trial: The Battle for Children and Custody*, I found that mothers who allege and can document sexual abuse are increasingly punished by losing custody of the child they are trying to protect. Many lawyers now advise mothers: "If it's true, don't allege it, or chances are you are going to lose custody." It's hard to convey the extent to which mothers are blamed, disparaged, feared, hated, belittled, and not believed in the American court system.

Marcia Rimland was a matrimonial lawyer; she knew what she was up against. She was distraught beyond measure, perhaps clinically insane. But she was also, objectively, trapped.

Let's consider why Rimland thought she had "no choice." Her simplest choice would have been to obey the court and permit her husband overnight visitation with four-year-old Abigail—an option she viewed as complying with and presiding over the slow destruction of her child.

Like many mothers, Rimland could have watched Abigail slowly come apart. Rimland could have denied what she believed was happening or denied that it was "that bad." Perhaps Abigail would "only" develop a multiple personality syndrome. Perhaps, like Hillary, Elizabeth Morgan's child, she would become actively suicidal. Perhaps, like Sherry

Neustein in another well-known case, Abigail would develop anorexia nervosa and begin to suffer from malnutrition. Perhaps Abigail would identify with her aggressor, blame her mother for not saving her, and become utterly lost in the fugue state we mistakenly call femininity. Perhaps Abigail would one day become a prostitute. Studies by sociologists and criminal justice researchers show that 80% to 90% of prostitutes have been victims of incest and childhood sexual abuse. If not a prostitute, then somebody clearly with a limited capacity to enjoy a quality life, with low self-esteem and with a good deal of self-hatred.

"The child could have survived it," some women have said to me, in macho voices. "We know women who have been through incest. What was the matter with Marcia Rimland? Was her kid better than everyone else's? I got though it, my neighbor's daughter got through it, we can all get through it. Now there's even treatment for incest."

Marcia Rimland decided that she would not accept this deal. She could not live if she turned her back on what so many of us learn to live with or minimize, namely, the sexual abuse of children by adult men.

Rimland's second option was to run away with her child—to go underground. But unlike Elizabeth Morgan, Rimland didn't have a father who was an ex-CIA operative with the will, know-how, and money to go undercover. Rimland had no living parents. There was nobody she could count on to take custody of the child if she got sent to jail. She had no support. Had she called me, I couldn't have done a thing for her. There is no "North" for women and children; there is no real underground—no sovereign feminist country for women (or men) in flight from sexual violence. Runaway mothers make it onto television documentaries, but they often lose custody of the kids and go to jail.

A third option: Rimland could have killed the alleged

abuser instead of herself and her child. But again, if Rimland shot Adler, who would raise her child? Rimland knew she would probably go to jail for a very long time. This is routinely what happens when battered women kill violent husbands or boyfriends—forget about men they're no longer living with. There have been some governors granting clemencies in these cases, but it's very rare.

Anyway, Rimland was probably a "nice" girl, and nice girls don't shoot men or cut off their penises. Nice girls usually turn their rage inward. They leave the place of unbearable pain by killing themselves, either slowly or suddenly.

So, from her point of view and mine, Rimland had no acceptable options. She was desperate. She knew the score. Like the heroine Sethe in Toni Morrison's novel *Beloved*, Marcia Rimland saw the slave catchers coming. She heard their breath hard on her heels and she refused to give up her daughter or herself.

Clearly, we need to provide more options for women like Rimland caught in the jaws of an unfeeling legal system. For a start, there should be an independent review of the Rimland–Adler case by judges, mental health professionals, and lawyers outside of Rockland County. Some very obvious, hard questions demand an answer:

Why didn't Judge Warren listen to the validator's report that sexual abuse had occurred? This validator interviewed both parents and the child. Why did Warren listen to a report that a second validator issued after not having interviewed anybody, which merely quibbled with the first validator's methodology? Why did the Appeals Court allow any unsupervised visitation between Adler and his daughter? Why did the D.A. in Rockland County not pursue the first validator's report of sexual abuse? What sort of political pressure, if any, was put on the judges involved in this case?

At the very least, Judge Warren should have erred on the

side of caution. He should have said, "Something is going on. I don't know what it is. Let's get more evaluations. Meanwhile, let's have neutral, trained personnel supervise the visits." The judge could have at least done that. The appellate level could have done that. I suspect they didn't because they never believed the mother or the first validator.

As a society, we are in denial about incest and other forms of male violence against women and children. Ironically, even as there are more books, articles, conferences, and first-hand survivor testimony about incest and molestation of children, it is more difficult for individual mothers to get a fair hearing. There seems to be a need to say, "Well maybe it's going on somewhere else out there—but not in my courtroom, not on this block, not next door to me, not in my marriage."

It's easier for us to blame the victim; to assume the mother is crazy, or exaggerating, or lying, or just being difficult. And a mother overwhelmed by fear that her child is being abused is not always a model of calm, restrained behavior. She may tremble and stutter in fear and in panic. She may cry or rage. And the judge may unthinkingly choose to believe a smooth, calm, rational—but not necessarily innocent—father.

Deep structural changes are required to combat the moral insanity that exists in courtrooms and lawyers' offices. Well-intentioned judges and mental health professionals are utterly unprepared to deal with allegations of child sexual abuse in any context, no less in the confusion of a custody battle. At best, they are seriously perplexed. In frustration, they "blame the victim" and "pass the buck" on to the next judge.

We must learn to handle child sexual abuse allegations differently: rapidly, very expertly, and with a cadre of specially trained professionals, not witch hunters. The trial and appeal process must be accelerated, and the child—as well as due process—protected at all costs. Psychiatry, psychology, and social work have not acquitted themselves nobly in this area. Therefore, interdisciplinary guidelines must be developed by a coalition of *feminist* grass-roots workers, scholars, and activists, many of whom are also psychiatrists, psychologists, and social workers. Such guidelines, or protocols, must be standardized, applied, and enforced everywhere.

While such within-the-system measures are being developed, we must dare to believe and shelter the "protective parent"—most often the mother. Marcia Rimland and her daughter might be alive today if they had had even a temporary escape hatch and some reason to hope for justice.

Some years ago, we began to blame mothers for not leaving men who abuse their children. And mothers began to blame themselves when they discovered many years later that their daughters had been sexually abused by husbands and fathers. Today, traditional women, who are not necessarily political or feminist, are saying no to sexual violence. They do not want their children to be sexually violated while they stand by and do nothing. They are desperate heroines. We need to make sure they have a way out.

NOTES

1. Two examples among many: Both Marc Lepine, the Montreal mass murderer of 14 young female engineering students, and Colin Thatcher, the wealthy Canadian legislator who for years battered his wife, Joanne Wilson, and then bludgeoned her to death (or perhaps hired someone to do it for him) in the midst of a bitter custody battle, were, as children, humiliated and beaten by their fathers. Both Lepine

and Thatcher also observed their fathers physically and verbally abuse their mothers. When boys are brutalized by their fathers, those who become violent often scapegoat women and children and *not* other men. Thus Lepine didn't shoot 14 fathers, nor did Thatcher murder—or procure the murder of—another man.

A Woman's Right to Self-Defense

The Case of Aileen Carol Wuornos

For the first time in U.S. history, a woman stands accused of being a serial killer: of having killed six adult male motorists, one by one, in just over a year, after accompanying them to wooded areas off Highway 75 in Florida, a state well known for its sun, surf, and serial killers.

I first heard about Aileen (Lee) Carol Wuornos in December of 1990, when Florida newspapers and national media announced:

> TWO WOMEN ARE BEING SOUGHT AS POSSIBLE SUSPECTS IN THE SHOOTING DEATHS OF EIGHT TO TWELVE MIDDLE AGED MEN WHO WERE LURED TO THEIR DEATHS ON THE FLORIDA HIGHWAYS. SUSPECT #1 IS A WHITE FEMALE, FIVE FEET EIGHT TO FIVE FEET TEN, WITH BLONDE HAIR, WHO IS TWENTY TO THIRTY YEARS OLD. SHE MAY HAVE A HEART TATTOO ON HER UPPER ARM. SUSPECT #2 IS ALSO A WHITE FEMALE, FIVE FEET FOUR TO FIVE FEET SIX, WITH A HEAVY BUILD AND SHORT BROWN HAIR. SHE MAY BE WEARING A BASEBALL CAP. THESE WOMEN ARE ARMED AND DANGEROUS AND MAY BE OUR NATION'S FIRST FEMALE SERIAL KILLERS.[1]

This sounded as diabolically whimsical as Orson Welles's 1938 broadcast on the Martian invasion. What was Everywoman's most forbidden fantasy and Everyman's worst nightmare doing on television? Was this some kind of joke? Perhaps these women were *feminist* Martians on a mission to avenge the Green River killings or the Montreal massacre. If not, did female serial killers really exist on earth?

Historically, women certainly have been convicted and executed[2] for killing adult male non-intimates, often with male accomplices, but sometimes alone, for money, "thrills," or revenge, in a drug-induced fit of rage, a battery-induced fugue state, and/or in death-defying self-defense.[3] Battered women have also killed male and family intimates, children, the elderly, and employers.[4] In Europe and elsewhere, warrior queens and female soldiers and civilians have killed their male counterparts in battle and in self-defense.[5] In the nineteenth and early twentieth centuries, female slaves and prostitutes sometimes injured or killed their masters, pimps, or johns, to avoid being beaten, raped, or killed, or because they *had* been seduced-and-abandoned, beaten, prostituted, or raped.[6]

However, according to contemporary studies[7] and countless true-crime accounts of homicide and femicide,[8] 99% of mass, sexual, and serial murder, and about 90% of all violent crime, is committed by men. Women do not massacre adult or male strangers, all at once, in large numbers, nor do they stalk-rape-and-kill male strangers, one by one. When those women who commit 10% of all violent crimes *do* kill, nearly half kill male intimates who have abused them or their children, and they invariably do so in self-defense.[9] Until recently, such (battered) women were viewed as more deviant and "crazy" than their male counterparts. Indeed, for a variety of reasons, female *victims* who kill male intimates in self-defense have been viewed more harshly than men who, unprovoked, kill their wives and girlfriends, or who kill female non-intimates, especially prostituted women.[10]

Most North American women prisoners have been convicted of petty economic crimes[11] and of primarily "female" crimes, such as prostitution.[12] Due to increased drug use and tougher drug penalties, more women are being imprisoned than ever before; however, women still comprise less than 6% of the North American prison population.[13] Nevertheless, this smaller and less violent population of female inmates (most of whom are young, uneducated, impoverished, African-American or Spanish-speaking single mothers) are, paradoxically, perceived as more violent than their more numerous and more violent male counterparts. Why?

Psychological Double Standards

Women are held to higher and different standards than men. People *expect* men to be violent; they are also carefully taught to deny or minimize male violence ("I don't believe any father would rape his own child") and to forgive violent men ("He's been under a lot of pressure," "He's willing to go into therapy"). On the other hand, people continue to *blame women* for male violence ("She must have liked rough sex if she stayed married to him," "She provoked him into beating her").

Also, people *do not* expect and will not permit women to be violent—not even in self-defense. (In fact, most people consistently confuse female self-defense with female aggression.) In addition, people demand that women, but not men, walk a very narrow tightrope of acceptable behaviors—perfectly, and with a smile.[14] And, until very recently, both men and women experienced woman's human nature (menstruation, menopause, pregnancy, aging, illness, odors, etc.) as unnatural, offensive, diseased. People still expect women to keep up an unnatural appearance—almost as a specifically female moral obligation.[15] Thus, most people are psychologically primed to distrust/dislike any woman who, in addition to being naturally imperfect, dares to commit other morally questionable acts. For women, such acts include having sex or children, for money, outside of marriage; or refusing to marry, bear, and rear a man's children; or abandoning responsibility for a child in a way that only men are allowed to do.

For example, while many people, including journalists, seemed to "hate" battered wife Hedda Nussbaum,[16] surrogate contract mother Mary Beth Whitehead,[17] and teenage prostitute Amy Fisher,[18] they remained emotionally "flat" about Joel Steinberg, William Stern, and, at least initially, about Joey Buttafuoco. Many, both male and female, also enjoyed "hating" Imelda Marcos[19] and Leona Helmsley[20] with a passion unvisited upon Ferdinand Marcos, Michael Milkin,[21] Ivan Boesky[22] and Neil Bush[23]—all of whose white collar (and other) crimes were far greater than Helmsley's. (Parenthetically, most people have felt enormous sympathy for Chief Justice Sol Wachtler,[24] little interest in his female victim, and utter revulsion for Bess Meyerson.[25])

These psychological double standards of perceived violence result in a double standard of punishment. In a way, such double standards already constitute punishment, as they poisonously permeate and circumscribe a woman's daily life. It doesn't stop here. Studies document that women are often punished more severely for lesser, primarily "female" crimes, such as prostitution, than men are for the more violent "male" crimes of femicide and homicide. When women commit "male" crimes such as spouse murder or stranger murder, in self-defense, or when they protectively kidnap a child, they are usually punished more harshly than their male so-called counterparts.[26]

According to the 1990 Florida State Supreme Court Gender Bias Report, "despite the perception that the criminal justice system is lenient to women...women [in Florida] are treated more harshly than similarly situated male offenders."[27] Generally, whatever their crime, men in jail and prison have greater access to libraries, educational and rehabilitation programs, modern gymnasiums, etc. than do women; men's jails are also more conveniently located for family visitation than are women's jails.[28]

To avoid jail overcrowding, male criminals are often plea-bargained into lesser sentences by prosecutors who fear they might otherwise be set free. Since women commit fewer crimes, there are fewer, less overcrowded, women's prisons, and less motivation to plea-bargain women out in order to save jail-space. Thus, women often inadvertently serve longer sentences for lesser crimes in more ramshackle jails than men serve for more serious crimes in more modern jails.[29] According to the findings of the 1990 Florida Gender Bias Report:

1. Women convicted of crimes have fewer opportunities for rehabilitation, training, and treatment throughout Florida.

2. There are currently only two maximum security state facilities for women. Minimum security inmates thus must endure conditions designed for maximum security inmates.

3. Some women's facilities fall below the requirements for exercise facilities and, in any event, are not comparable to those provided for men.

4. Women generally are imprisoned for less serious offenses than their male counterparts

[and] have significantly limited access to alternative programs or rehabilitative treatment. Men have programs and alternative treatment centers throughout Florida.

5. In the county jails, overcrowding in the male population results in men being released. However, there is less overcrowding among women inmates. As a result, women serve longer sentences than men who have committed more serious crimes.

6. Women have limited access to trusteeships and work release programs in comparison to men, thus restricting the availability of early release for good behavior.

7. Women sentenced to work release by the courts nevertheless are often incarcerated because of the lack of work release programs or the shortage of openings in similar programs for women.

8. Women unable to participate in work release programs lack the opportunity to gain useful work experience. This results in less successful reentry into society after incarceration and more time spent incarcerated than similarly situated male offenders.

9. Men are favored in experimental and alternative programs around Florida.

10. The remote location of some jails for women restricts family visitation, access to counsel, and information.[30]

Another example: as noted, battered women who kill in self-defense account for about half of all women who kill. Even here, men and women are not "equal." (Non-battered) men kill their female domestic partners three to four times more often than (battered) women kill their domestic partners/agressors. Battered women who kill in self-defense rarely "get off" and, to date, are rarely granted clemency; most are given long or even life sentences.[31]

In comparison, minority/immigrant men are sometimes freed on the grounds that, in their culture, men are "obligated" to kill wives who want to desert their whipping-girl posts to go to work, go to school, or get a divorce. White male defendants have sometimes successfully claimed that their wives' desire to "shop too much" or to leave the marriage amounted to unbearable sexual humiliation.[32]

In addition, while men accused of murder often refuse to confess, women, who believe that the criminal justice system will "care about" the "truth," are all too eager to "tell all," especially if they've killed their batterers or kidnapped their children to protect them from paternal physical and sexual abuse. Women are routinely punished for their naiveté and honesty, and/or for their inability or refusal to play courtroom "war games."[33]

Judges, jurors, Senate Judiciary Committee members, and We, the People, still value men's lives more highly than women's and feel compassion for male—but not for female—sinners. When a woman is accused of committing a crime (and even when the woman is the *crime-victim*), her story is rarely believed, by men or by other women, and even less so if she's accusing a man of being the aggressor. That's when she's Anita Hill or Patricia Bowman; imagine what happens when she's a prostituted woman, armed robber, child-beater, or cold killer. Few are "interested" in hearing her "excuses": that she was a battered wife, a serial rape and/or incest victim, or that she killed in self-defense.

What do we really know about women killers—especially those who kill male non-intimates?

Women Killers In Literature, Film, and the Social Sciences

Have Austen, the Brontes, Eliot, Woolf, Colette, Wharton, Stein, Barnes, Nin, de Beauvoir, or Lessing ever given us a portrait of homicidal fury in female form? I don't think so, but neither have Dostoevski, Melville, Baudelaire, Zola, Dickens, Celine, Genet, Camus, Burroughs, Miller, Wright, Ellison, Mailer, Mishima, or Capote. Few pre-feminist writers have ever dared to imagine the lives of women killers and outlaws.[34]

Not one character comes to mind: no female Raskolnikov, Meursault, or Bigger Thomas. How could so many great writers have resisted this temptation?

Perhaps it wasn't challenging enough. Until recently—and I'm not sure much has changed—women and men of color were already presumed guilty, inferior, even evil, by virtue of their gender and skin-color, and were supposed to be humbled and punished. There's no story here. On the other hand, white men were presumed innocent, Godlike, heroic, both by birth and in the courtroom. Their descent into evil, redemption, or lack of it—now that's a story!

This may be changing. Something's up, it's in the air, it's a sea-change, and suddenly, or so it seems, we are being bombarded by celluloid images of women killing men: Barbra Streisand's incest-victim prostitute in *Nuts*; the three women who stomp a man to death in the Dutch film *A Question of Silence*; and the battered wives and victims of rape in *The Burning Bed*, *Sleeping with the Enemy*, *Mortal Thoughts*, and *Thelma and Louise*. Superficially, nontraditional and career-women who kill men are also beginning to appear in films such as *Silence of the Lambs*, *Alien One* and *Two*, *Terminator Two*, *La Femme Nikita*, *Basic Instinct*, *Patriot Games*, *Passenger 57*, etc.

In actuality, these images have feminist precursors. By 1979-80, the pre-existing grassroots shelter movement for battered women, and feminist lawyers and social scientists such as Angela Browne (1987),[35] Cynthia Gillespie (1989),[36] Ann Jones (1985),[37] Susan Schechter (1982),[38] Elizabeth Schneider (1978),[39] Diana Russell and Nicole Van den Ven (1976),[40] and Lenore Walker (1979, 1989)[41] began to focus on battered women who kill.[42]

Earlier still, and at a more imaginative level, feminist writers began to portray heroic, or anti-heroic, women who kill: Monique Wittig's fictionalized band of Amazon warriors, set in the future, in *Les Guerilleres* (1969),[43] and Manastabal, her lesbian feminist Archangel, who guides Wittig through a surrealistic Purgatory of abused women in *Across the Acheron* (1985);[44] Nawal el Sadawi's Firdaus, a prostituted woman who kills her pimp in *Woman at Point Zero* (1975);[45] Joanna Russ's Janet Evason, an advanced extra-terrestrial who kills heroically and in self-defense, in *The Female Man* (1976);[46] Marge Piercy's Connie Ramos, a time-traveler and ideological warrior, in *Woman on the Edge of Time* (1976);[47] Suzy McKee Charnes's warriors in *Mother-Lines* (197);[48] Sally Gearheart's lesbian feminist warriors in *The Wanderground* (1976);[49] Kate Millett's Gertrude Baniszewski, who, in real life, led a gang of teenagers in the torture-killing of 16-year-old Sylvia Likens, in *The Basement—Meditations on a Human Sacrifice* (1979);[50] Margaret Atwood's Ofglen, an ideological warrior who mercifully kills a male comrade to spare him a slow and agonizing death in *The Handmaid's Tale* (1985);[51] Jeanette Winterson's Dog Woman, who is given to killing Puritans with an ax during the reign of Charles the Second in *Sexing the Cherry*

(1989);[52] Helen Zahavi's Bella, an ex-prostitute, "no one special," but someone who, once she'd "realized she'd had enough," proceeds to kill at least seven sexually and murderously assaultive men, in *The Weekend* (1991);[53] and Diana Rivers's band of lesbian feminist psychic-military warriors in *Daughters of the Great Star* (1992)[54]. Andrea Dworkin's *Mercy*,[55] first published in England in 1990 and in the United States in 1991, reads like something the visionary Cassandra might have written—had she escaped her life as Agamemnon's slave-prostitute and turned military tactician, had she escaped from History and become an "avenging angel":

> We surge through the sex dungeon where our kind are kept, the butcher shops where our kind are sold; we break them loose; Amnesty International will not help us, the United Nations will not help us; so at night, ghosts, we convene; to spread justice...I am an apprentice: sorcerer or assassin or vandal or vigilante; or avenger; I am in formation as the new one who will emerge.[56]

Women, including women writers, have been conditioned to be the social enforcers of the status quo, to challenge and condemn any woman (or man) who "steps out of line." That women have begun to imagine and befriend women killers—and in print—is very promising. Writers need to create female heroes and anti-heroes, larger than life. Acts of radical compassion are required, acts that embrace other women, not just "nice" girls or "perfect" victims, not when it's safe, but precisely when it's risky.

Enter Aileen (Lee) Carol Wuornos—a prostitute and lesbian convicted of killing four men and accused of killing at least two more—a really "bad" girl.

Is Wuornos a Serial Killer?

The media and social scientists have described Wuornos as the first "female serial killer"; the FBI has *classified* her as such. But is this true? Is Wuornos indeed a female "Jack the Ripper," "Hillside Strangler," "Green River Killer," or "Night-Stalker"? Eric Hickey, sociologist and criminologist, estimated that there has been an average of at least five serial killers each year in the United States since 1970. The vast majority are men (approximately 170 between 1970 and 1988). Hickey estimated that in the nearly 200 years between 1800 and 1988, a total of 34 female serial killers have existed—contrasted with an estimated 30 male serial killers on the loose as of the late 1980s. A disproportionate number of serial killing victims are women, a trend which Hickey says may be increasing.[57]

Serial killers are mainly white male drifters, obsessed with pornography and woman-hatred, who sexually use their victims, either before or after killing them, and who were themselves *paternally* abused children. As adults, they scapegoat not fathers but mainly women, sometimes children, sometimes male homosexuals—who are seen as "feminine" or vulnerable. Serial killers may be responsible for the daily, and permanent, disappearance of thousands of prostituted and non-prostituted women, each and every year, all across the United States.[58] In addition, most sex-murderers who stalk, rape, torture, and kill prostitutes (and non-prostitutes, whom they view as prostitutes and as therefore worthy of death), are rarely ever found or convicted.[59]

I don't think Wuornos fits this description. Wuornos was not a pornography addict, she did not eroticize her hatred of women (or of men); she did not stalk women, or male or female prostitutes; in fact, she *was* a prostituted woman. The men she killed all fit the profile of johns, those who frequent prostitutes.

In addition, most serial killers don't insist that they killed in self-defense—as Wuornos has. She said so at least 50 times during her three-hour, videotaped, psychologically manipulated confession on January 16, 1991, in which she also said that she believed she was going to be beaten or raped or killed by each of her victims.[60]

People say that Wuornos could not have killed *six times* in self defense, that no one could—except of course men, in times of war. But Wuornos, a seriously abused child and a serially raped and beaten teenage and adult prostitute, has been under attack all her life, probably more than any soldier in any real war.

In my opinion, Wuornos's testimony in the first trial was both moving and credible as she described being verbally threatened, tied up and then brutally raped, both anally and vaginally, by Richard Mallory.[61] According to Wuornos, this is what Richard Mallory did to her on the night of November 30th, 1989:

> I went to Tampa and made a little money hustling. I was hitchhiking home at night. This guy picked me up right outside of Tampa, underneath the bridge. So he's smokin' pot and we're goin' down the road and he says, 'Do you want a drink?' So we're drinkin' and we're gettin' pretty drunk. Then, around 5:00 in the morning, he says: 'Okay, do you want to make your money now?' So we go into the woods. He's huggin' and kissin' on me. He starts pushin' me down. And I said, 'Wait a minute, you know, get cool. You don't have to get rough, you know. Let's have fun.'[62]
>
> I said I would not [have sex with him]. 'Yes, you are, bitch. You're going to do everything I tell you. If you don't, I'm going to kill you and [have sex with you] after you're dead just like the other sluts. It doesn't matter, your body will still be warm.' He tied my wrists to the steering wheel, and screwed me in the ass.

Afterwards, he got a Visine bottle filled with rubbing alchohol out of the trunk. He said the visine bottle was one of my surprises. He emptied it into my rectum. It really hurt bad because he tore me up a lot. He got dressed, got a radio, sat on the hood for what seemed like an hour. I was really pissed. I was yelling at him, and struggling to get my hands free. Eventually he untied me, put a stereo wire around my neck and tried to rape me again.[63]

Then I thought to myself, well, this dir...this dirty bastard deserves to die anyway because of what he was tryin' to do to me. We struggled. I reached for my gun. I shot him. I scrambled to cover the shooting because I didn't think the police would believe I killed him in self-defense.[64]

I have to say it, that I killed 'em all because they got violent with me and I decided to defend myself. I wasn't gonna let 'em beat the shit outta me or kill me, either. I'm sure if after the fightin' they found I had a weapon, they would've shot me. So I just shot them. [65]

Apart from her own testimony, the jury never got to hear any evidence about violence toward prostitutes in general, or about Mallory's history of violence toward women in particular, that might have helped them evaluate Wuornos's much-derided claim of self-defense.

Violence Against Prostitutes

There is a suppressed, forgotten, and/or unrecorded history of violence against prostituted women both world-wide and in North America. Prostitutes have long been considered "fair game" for sexual harassment, rape, gang-rape, "kinky" sex, robbery, and beatings; their homes have been destroyed, they have been taunted, even killed, for "sport."[66] According to historian Timothy J. Gilfoyle,

After 1820, physical violence against prostitutes [in New York City] increased dramatically.

...Drunken, disorderly, and delirious males often became incensed when a prostitute or madam denied them their heart's desire.[67]

...The increasing frequency of these attacks during the 1830s reflected, in part, the growing perception that prostitutes were fair game for the aggressions of frustrated males. The most threatening form of assault was "the spree" or "row." Fueled by male camaraderie and substantial quantities of liquor, gangs of rampaging drunks moved from one saloon or brothel to another, becoming increasingly obnoxious and violent at every stop.... Many sprees evolved into scenes of sadistic terror.[68]

...Just as some white men terrorized black proprietors of small businesses, oyster shops, churches, and theaters, others found the increased economic and social power of prostitutes threatening.

...Efforts to limit accessibility, in the mind of the brothel bully, violated custom and male prerogative.

...In 1836, for example, John Chichester and his politically connected gang attacked at least three bordellos. Entering Jane Ann Jackson's Chapel Street brothel with bats, they destroyed windows and shutters and threatened to cut Miss Jackson's throat. Chichester's consorts then broke into Eliza Ludlow's house and forced her to serve brandy; they concluded their guzzling by tossing the glasses in the fire. Then they "abused the inmates of the house," burned a rug, broke a bench by hurling it at a prostitute, and threatened to toss one woman out the window.[69]

...Just as lynchings in the American South later in the century extended psychological control far beyond their immediate victims, brothel riots probably imposed similar behavioral constraints upon prostitutes.[70]

A 1991 study by the Council for Prostitution Alternatives,[71] in Portland, Oregon, documented that 78% of 55 prostituted women reported being raped an average of 16 times annually by their pimps and 33 times a year by johns.[72] Twelve rape complaints were made in the criminal justice system and neither pimps nor johns were ever convicted. These prostitutes also reported being "horribly beaten" by their pimps an average of 58 times a year.[73] The frequency of beatings by pimps ranged from once to daily, or 365 times per year; the frequency of beatings by johns ranged from 1 to 400 times a year. Legal action was pursued in 13 cases, resulting in two convictions for "aggravated assault." Fifty-three percent were the victims of sexual torture at the hands of both pimps and johns; nearly a third reported being mutilated as a result of this torture.[74] Legal action was sought in eight cases and only once was a pimp convicted.

The 1990 Florida Supreme Court Gender Bias Report stated that "[p]rostitution is not a victimless crime.... Prostitute rape is rarely reported, investigated, prosecuted or taken seriously...[a]lmost all young prostitutes have run away from sexual and physical abuse in their homes...[and]...are most often the victims of coercion."[75] According to Philippa Levine, who studied street prostitutes in Florida,

> [t]he same dangers attached to prostitution wherever I looked. In every [Florida] city and town I heard grim stories of violence and coercion, of rape and murder, of non-payment and forced sex, of hunger, pain, disease, and desperation.
>
> ...[W]e should not forget the still unsolved murders of young prostitutes in Pensacola, the crack-addicted street-walkers of Tallahassee, the heroin-addicted HIV-infected woman whose prostitution charges made headlines in Tampa [in 1988] and whose name was disclosed by the media with little care for her health or dignity.[76]

...[T]he [Florida] police confirmed that they knew of no [prostitutes] who had not had bad experiences with customers. Intimate transactions with strangers constitute danger in themselves, all the more so when one considers that almost all street prostitution is conducted in parked cars controlled by those customers. Women spoke of jumping out of moving cars in preference to facing weapons, of being driven to lonely areas against their will, of non-paying clients whose violent behaviour forced them to comply with unanticipated desires. One interviewee described one horrific night when three separate clients threatened her with a knife.[77]

Research has also indicated that street and juvenile prostitutes suffer bruises, broken bones, and very poor health as a result of multiple beatings and rape.[78] According to Eleanor Miller, "The beatings and sexual assaults female hustlers received at the hands of their 'men,' their 'dates,' their wives-in-law, former 'women' of their 'men,' and other street people as well as the police, were numerous and often brutal."[79] Underage girls are often introduced into prostitution by family intimates who either rape and then begin selling them, or "only" rape them, often from the time they are seven or eight years old; in so doing, they fatally break their spirits, and drive them out of the house and into the arms of waiting pimps and johns, often by the time they are twelve or thirteen years old.[80] According to Susan Kay Hunter, Executive Director of Council for Prostitution Alternatives,

Suicide is common among victim/survivors of prostitution: 75% of women victimized by escort prostitution have attempted suicide and prostituted women comprise 15% of all suicides reported by hospitals.[81]

According to a 1981 study, 78% of 200 street prostituted women, the majority of whom were under 21 years of age, reported being victimized by forced perversion an average of 16.6 times each woman; 70% were victimized by john rape (when johns went beyond what was agreed on) an average of 31 times; 74% were victimized by non-payment an average of five times; 65% were victims of violence an average of nine times; 41% were victimized in some other way such as being forced into sex for no pay with police, beaten by police, or beaten by other prostitutes.[82] Additionally, 65% of these young streetwalkers were physically abused and beaten by customers an average of four times—because they "got off on it, enjoyed it and thought it was part of sex," or because the customers hated prostitutes or hated women in general.[83]

Prostituted women often make headlines when their headless and mutilated bodies are discovered. To date,

> At least forty-eight women, mainly prostitutes, were killed by the Green River Killer; up to thirty-one women [were] murdered in Miami over a three year period, most of them prostitutes; fourteen in Denver; twenty-nine in Los Angeles; seven in Oakland. Forty-three in San Diego; fourteen in Rochester; eight in Arlington, Virginia; nine in New Bedford, Massachusetts, seventeen in Alaska, ten in Tampa. Three girls, ages 3, 4, and 6, [were] sold in Suffolk, New York. Three prostitutes were reported dead in Spokane, Washington in 1990, leading some to speculate that the "Green River" murderer of 48 women and girls had once again become "active."
>
> ...[W]omen in prostitution are dying quickly. One authority cited in the Canadian Report on Prostitution and Pornography concluded that women and girls in prostitution suffer a mortality rate 40 times the national average.[84]

Wuornos's public defenders, Trish Jenkins and Ed Bonnett, chose not to use any of the pro bono expert witnesses I'd gathered together who were ready to testify for the defense in the first trial. In my view, such experts were needed to educate the jury about the routine and horrendous violence against prostituted women, including Wuornos, the long-term consequences of extreme trauma,[85] and a woman's right to self-defense.[86]

If the people on Wuornos's jury had been allowed to hear from such experts, perhaps, just perhaps, they'd have been better able to understand that, as Wuornos has said, she lived "on dangerous ground at all times," and that she killed Richard Mallory in self-defense.[87] For example, in addition to Mallory's drunken sadism, Wuornos's early childhood—and the fact that she was serially raped and abused all her life—predisposed her to both deny and to overreact to all subsequent abuse.[88]

We know that Wuornos never met her father, Leo Pitman, a man who was imprisoned for molesting one child and who possibly murdered another, a man who committed suicide in prison when Wuornos was 13; that Wuornos's teen-age mother, Diane, abandoned her when Wuornos was a toddler; and that her maternal grandparents took her in. Wuornos was physically, psychologically, and probably sexually abused, as well as seriously neglected at home. She was badly scarred in a fire when she was nine; her life-long hearing impairment was never corrected. We also know that Wuornos was raped, presumably by a stranger, when she was 12, impregnated, and sent to a home for unwed mothers, where she gave birth to a son she surrendered for adoption.

We know that Wuornos's maternal grandmother was an alcoholic who died of liver failure in 1971, when Wuornos was 14; that Wuornos finally ran away from home shortly thereafter; and that in her first year as a runaway, she was reportedly beaten and raped at least six times by six different men.

We know that Wuornos's grandfather killed himself in 1976, the year her brother Keith died of cancer, and that Wuornos tried to commit suicide, at least once seriously, by shooting herself in the stomach. Like many female victims of serious childhood abuse, Wuornos became an alcoholic, a prostitute, and a petty thief. She supported herself as a prostitute as she drifted between Michigan and Florida from 1971 to 1991. Wuornos spent time in reform school in Michigan and in jail in Florida.

Let's assume that Wuornos's attorneys decided not to use any pro bono experts. What else might they have done? If a prostituted woman (or anyone) alleges rape and self-defense, and there are no eye-witnesses other than the accused, it is appropriate to review the murdered man's past history of violence toward both prostitutes and non-prostitutes.[89]

Shortly after the Mallory homicide, *and a month before Wuornos's arrest*, Mallory's former girlfriend, Jackie Davis, gave a grim portrayal of Mallory to investigator Larry Horzepa. Mallory, Ms. Davis recounted, had served ten years in prison for burglary, suffered from severe mood swings, drank too much, was violent to women, enjoyed the strip bars, was "into" pornography, and had undergone therapy for some kind of sexual dysfunction.[90] A search of Mallory's business revealed that he was erratic in business, heavily in debt, in trouble with the IRS, and had received many hostile letters from angry customers.[91] (Ultimately, Judge Uriel Blount did not allow Jackie Davis to testify about Mallory's past violence toward women.)

However, the prosecution did not share Davis's information with the defense for more than a year. The prosecution revealed this information on January 10th, 1992, three days before Wuornos was to stand trial for Mallory's murder. On January 10th, Judge Blount denied a defense motion for the admission of this testimony at trial and for a continuance to allow the defense to find and question Davis anew.[92] In my view, the absence of such corroborating evidence was absolutely damaging to Wuornos' self-defense claim.

Chastity Lee Marcus, a Tampa-based exotic dancer, prostituted woman, and member of the Sons of Silence Motorcycle gang, was interviewed by the police as possibly the last person to have seen Mallory alive.[93] Marcus described Mallory as a drinking and partying man who thought nothing of paying $600 (or the equivalent in VCRs) to have sex with two prostitutes at once: herself and her friend "Danielle."[94]

Neither the defense nor the prosecution questioned Marcus, Mallory's ex-wife, or another ex-girlfriend, Nancy Peterson, about Mallory's violence toward them or toward other women. Neither Jackie Davis, Chastity Lee Marcus, nor Nancy Peterson ever testified for the defense.[95]

It is true that Wuornos's public defender, Trish Jenkins, asked for a continuance at the last moment, in order to question Davis. However, on October 15, 1991—*two months before the trial started*—Jenkins herself had deposed Officer Lawrence Horzepa about Jackie Davis.[96] Perhaps Jenkins forgot about this deposition. In a series of meetings with Jenkins, held in April and May of 1991—*nearly seven months before the first trial*—feminists, myself included, had asked Jenkins and her investigator, Don Sanchez, to look into Mallory's past.[97] They never did. A routine computer check would have revealed that Richard Mallory had done many years in Patuxent Prison, in Maryland, as a sex offender. In Mallory's criminal record he was described as an "impulsive and explosive individual who will get into serious difficulty, most likely of a sexual nature.... Because of his emotional disturbance and his poor control of his sexual impulses, he could present a potential danger to his environment in the future."[98]

I eventually hired Marion County ex-police officer Brian Jarvis, who had initially worked on the Wuornos case, to conduct a computer search and a series of interviews about Mallory. NBC private investigator Jack Kassewitz also learned of Mallory's criminal record and on November 10, 1992, NBC-Dateline aired the above findings. NBC also revealed that the defense had failed to call a number of "friendly" witnesses.[99]

It is not clear whether the prosecution had ever done a thorough computer check on Mallory, or whether they actively suppressed the results. Prosecutor John Tanner admitted, on camera, that the prosecution's preparation had been "incomplete."[100] He also admitted that "we may have to try the case again."[101]

The Psycho-Pathology of Woman-Hatred

Wuornos may have had sex for money with a "guesstimated" quarter of a million men. Did the six johns she killed demand something that so terrorized and outraged her that she "snapped"? Or was it just the first of the six, Richard Mallory, john number quarter-million-plus-one, who sent her over the edge?

Was a quarter-million johns all Wuornos could take before she cracked, or, dare I say it, experienced a momentary flight into sanity? Was a quarter-million johns all Wournos could take before she decided that "enough was enough"?

Was it anything like the Dutch film, *A Question of Silence*,[102] in which five women, strangers to each other, are shopping in the same store on the very day each woman, finally, has had enough of being treated like a "woman" by men? In a rather dreamlike sequence, three of the women spontaneously stomp to death the 250,001st man who treats them with contempt; and they do so without exchanging a word. After the women are arrested, they maintain an uncanny silence.

The prison psychiatrist, a "happily married" woman, hopes to save them by finding them insane. To her consternation, she can find nothing wrong with them. They are all ordinary, rather "nice" women who are not insane. With considerable anguish, the psychiatrist acknowledges that there is a war going on against women and that during war, atrocities are committed—usually by the stronger, occupying force; more rarely, by the occupied themselves. Perhaps, she thinks, women are only insane when they put up with the daily atrocities committed against them, or when they deny that such atrocities are really happening. Improbably, the psychiatrist joins the silent, imprisoned women and their silent female supporters—none of whom expect justice or understanding.

A *Question of Silence* is a surrealistic feature film.

Wuornos's story—especially since her arrest on January 9, 1991—is far more surrealistic.

Despite widespread media attention, the state of Florida treated Wuornos the way it treats all its female prisoners— very badly. As a pre-trial detainee, Wuornos was entitled to the presumption of innocence. She was, instead, punished before her first trial. She lost more than 40 pounds and appeared to age ten years within ten months. Wuornos was kept in solitary confinement—intermittently, and sometimes without her clothes (presumably as a way of preventing her suicide). She was also verbally abused and threatened by prison guards and other inmates, deprived of daylight and exercise, allowed no safe, monitored medication for withdrawal from her long-standing alcohol addiction, and denied all contact visits. Wuornos did place numerous collect phone calls to Arlene Pralle, the Born-Again Christian "Good Samaritan" who first began writing to her in February of

1991, and who legally adopted her in November of 1991.

Wuornos was kept in jail at an eight-hour-round-trip distance from her public defender, Trish Jenkins. Therefore, their visits were not as frequent as Wuornos might have wished (or needed).[103] In addition, although Wuornos could not hear or see very well, her frequent requests for a hearing aid and for glasses were denied, as was permission to see a gynecologist for painful, heavy bleeding. Trish Jenkins finally ordered a gynecological consultation in December of 1991, but only after I called some Florida newspapers about Wuornos's (routine) mistreatment in jail.[104] I suggested that Wuornos's mistreatment was a sadistic and calculated attempt to destroy her capacity to participate in her own trial and, perhaps, to drive her to suicide. I questioned whether Wuornos could receive a fair trial on these grounds alone.[105]

Wuornos decided to confess only after repeated entreaties by Tyria Moore, her lover, who was, early on, herself a suspect in the police investigation. Moore cooperated with the police by taping a number of phone calls from Wuornos in jail in which Moore begged Wuornos to protect her. During her videotaped confession, Wuornos kept explaining that she was only confessing in order to save Moore.

In her videotaped confession, Wuornos was visibly distraught, confused, and rambling. Her police interrogators created a false sense of camaraderie with her by frequent inquiries as to her comfort and by cozy small talk. Wuornos seemed to have no clear understanding of where she was, whether she was talking to police officers or lawyers, why exactly she needed a lawyer, or what exactly a lawyer could do for her. Despite the fact that she was going through alcohol withdrawal, scared, and pressured by Moore into confessing, Wuornos continued to insist that the killings were done in self-defense.[106] The absence of skilled legal counsel—even after Wuornos said she wanted counsel—was woefully apparent. Late in the session, counsel finally arrived.

Some of the events Wuornos attempted to describe to the police in her confession on January 16, 1991 had happened more than a year before; any clear recollection she might have been able to conjure up was distorted, manipulated, or not properly "heard" by her interrogators. As a result, Wournos omitted important details. Her later, more detailed account at trial, describing the horrific abuse she suffered at Mallory's hands immediately preceding his homicide, was viewed as "inconsistent," "contradictory," or as a series of "lies."

The Media Connection

Even before Wuornos was arrested, local, national, and international media, including Hollywood and network TV filmmakers, became part of the drama. The most (routinely) brazen manipulation of Wuornos (and of her case) commenced. For example, right after her arrest, Wuornos's first public defender, Ray Cass, helped Wuornos negotiate a deal with Hollywood filmmaker Jacqui Giroux—the only person who visited Wuornos immediately following her arrest. Three Marion County sheriffs—Major Dan Henry, Sergeant Bruce Munster, and Captain Steve Binegar—together with Wuornos's ex-lover, Tyria Moore, allegedly sold *their* version of the story to CBS/Republic Pictures.[107] (Tyria Moore was granted immunity in exchange for her testimony against Wuornos.)[108] Arlene Pralle and Wuornos's third attorney, Steve Glazer, negotiated with and pocketed the relatively small amounts of money paid by the media to interview Wuornos on Death Row. In a phone conversation, Glazer himself confirmed to me that Montel Williams, BBC, and Geraldo Rivera each paid between $7,500 and $10,000 to interview Wuornos on Death Row.[109] Glazer also persuaded

Wuornos to withdraw her lawsuit against Giroux and to renegotiate (or "upgrade") the contract instead.[110]

Although the media proved as much hero as villain, Government by Geraldo, if not translated into a series of legal motions, is at best useless and at worse harmful. For example, Wuornos's original judge, Gayle Graziano, replaced Wuornos's first public defender, Ray Cass—who Wuornos charged had negotiated with Hollywood producer Jacqui Giroux for the movie rights to Wuornos's story. At Wuornos's request, her new public defender was a woman: Trish Jenkins of neighboring Marion County. This replacement (of a man and by a female lawyer in another county) was ultimately used by the prosecution to force Graziano, reportedly a feminist, into recusing herself.[111]

Another example: According to a number of people I interviewed, Giroux allegedly began offering contracts for $5,000 to the people in Wuornos's childhood if they spoke only to Giroux—and presumably not to any other media person.[112] For this and other reasons, some Michigan residents who knew how badly Wuornos had been abused during childhood allegedly did not cooperate with Wuornos's public defenders at all, or in a timely fashion. When Giroux allegedly tried to intercede, it was too late. In any event, Trish Jenkins did not call anyone to testify for the defense from Michigan or elsewhere.

Double Standards for Serial Killers?

Do we have different standards for evil, violence, and insanity: one for men, another for women? Or is Wuornos simply *too* evil, for a woman? As such, is her punishment a warning to other women that female violence, including self-defense, will never be glamorized or forgiven, only punished—swiftly and terribly?

One reporter I spoke to about the Wuornos case kept

needling me for not being cynical enough: "C'mon, Wuornos is not entitled to the kind of lawyer that William Kennedy Smith or Mike Tyson had. Get real!" But what does it mean that Jeffrey Dahmer, accused of torturing, raping, killing, cannibalizing, and dismembering 15 young men, mainly of color—none of whom attacked him—was able to command a private lawyer, some well-known national experts, his father and stepmother, and continuous live TV in the courtroom? In addition, skinheads apparently demonstrated on his behalf in Chicago ("He got rid of the filth" they chanted), and a growing number of women supporters filled the courtroom, some of whom reportedly formed a Jeffrey Dahmer Fan Club.[113]

Or, let's look at another Florida serial killer: Ted Bundy, who killed at least 30 (and possibly 100) women.[114] Several lawyers, including Atlanta lawyer Millard Farmer and North Florida lawyer Brian T. Hays, offered to defend Bundy pro bono in Florida; Dr. Emil Spillman advised him on jury selection pro bono; at one point, no fewer than five public defenders assisted Bundy, who insisted on representing himself.[115]

Even more interesting is that the State of Florida offered Bundy a life sentence without parole, a plea bargain Bundy refused. Jenkins et al. tried to arrange a similar plea for Wuornos but James Russell, the Dixie County Prosecutor, thought Wuornos deserved to die and refused to agree to a plea bargain.

Considering its complexity, Wuornos's first trial was exceptionally brief: it took only 13 court days. The State had estimated that the trial would last from three to six weeks. Judge Blount, who was coaxed out of retirement to replace Judge Graziano, granted all of the prosecution and denied most of the defense motions. In deference to the State's motion, the jury was allowed to see excerpts from Wuornos's videotaped confession—*minus* her repeated statements that she killed in self-defense. Under Florida's *Williams* rule,[116] the jury was also permitted to hear similar fact evidence from the six other alleged murders. (Under the same *Williams* rule, Judge Mary Lupo, presiding in William Kennedy Smith's 1991 Palm Beach rape trial, did not allow the jury to hear any of the other allegations of rape against Smith.[117])

Judge Blount did not grant the defense a change of venue despite the enormous local, pre-trial publicity, which included Wuornos's televised confession. (Ted Bundy did get a change of venue, from Tallahassee to Miami, for similar reasons). Judge Blount felt that he could seat an "impartial" jury even if they'd seen or heard about the confession—and he did so in a day and a half!

Given the gravity and the notoriety of the case, the 68 prospective jurors might have been polled individually; none were. Further, only jurors who said they believed in the death penalty were seated. (This is routinely done in Florida.[118])

During the guilt/innocence phase of this bifurcated capital trial, Wuornos herself was the *only* witness for the defense. As previously noted, early in the trial preparation, feminists, myself included, contacted more than 50 experts, approximately ten of whom agreed to testify for the defense, pro bono or at minimal cost. These included a psychologist, a psychiatrist, experts in prostitution and violence against prostitutes, experts in child abuse, battery, rape trauma syndrome, lesbianism, lesbian battery, female alcoholism, and the psychology of adoption. None of these experts—and no other experts with similar information—were ever called by the defense. Three weeks before the trial, Trish Jenkins called *one* of these experts for the first time, but never called her back.[119] As previously noted, Wuornos was the only one who took the stand on her own behalf, a dubious strategy considering her vulnerability to impeachment.

The prosecution's legal theory was replete with misogynist stereotypes: lead prosecutor John Tanner, a Born-Again Christian, had been Ted Bundy's deathrow "minister" and had tried to have Bundy's execution delayed.[120] In his opening and closing arguments, Tanner portrayed Wuornos as a "predatory prostitute" whose "appetite for lust and control had taken a lethal turn," who "had been exercising control for years over men," and who "killed for power, for full and ultimate control."[121]

In the penalty phase of the trial, the jury heard from defense psychologists Elizabeth McMahon and Harry Krop, two experts more experienced in testifying for *male* killers than for female killers on trial. According to McMahon: "Lee [Wuornos] is such a classic textbook example of a borderline personality . . . . she calls almost everybody a 'fucker.' I don't know that Wuornos can get a sentence out without that . . . she is a child, developmentally and emotionally."[122] Krop also diagnosed Wuornos as a "borderline personality" suffering from "organic dysfunction in the brain cortex."[123]

The defense presented no family members or friends in mitigation. Many of Wuornos's childhood relatives and friends either were never asked to testify for the defense; were asked but never called; or allegedly were, in their view, *paid* to keep silent by Hollywood producer Jacqui Giroux.

When men are accused of crimes, even terrible crimes, their families invariably back them. The wives of the "Big Dan" gang-rapists in New Bedford, Massachusetts, the Kennedy women, Mike Tyson's adoptive mother, the families of the young men accused and exonerated in the gang-rape of a St. John's University student, and those of the gang-rapists of a young woman with an IQ of 64 in Glen Ridge, New Jersey, all stood by their men.

Even Ted Bundy had enormous emotional and secretarial/public-relations support from his mother, Louise, and from his 32-year-old "fiancee" Carol Ann Boone, whom he would marry and later impregnate. Both Louise and Carol Ann testified for Bundy. Scores of young women attended the trial and openly flirted with Bundy in court.[124]

Impoverished (and non-impoverished) women do not usually have anyone willing to speak for them, nor do they routinely have "supportive" families. They're lucky if they don't die at the hands of a family intimate. Often, the families of female outlaws are the ones who turn them in and testify against them. Wuornos's lesbian ex-lover, Tyria Moore, was the star prosecution witness against her. Wuornos's uncle, 12 years her senior, with whom she'd been raised as a sibling, and whom she hadn't seen for at least 20 years, testified for the *prosecution*. He claimed that Wuornos had never been abused at home and therefore had no "reason" to kill anyone.[125]

Wuornos did have the support of Arlene Pralle, the woman who contacted Wuornos after her arrest and who is now her legal mother. Pralle accepted countless collect calls from Wuornos in jail, and facilitated countless telephone interviews between Wuornos and the media by inviting the journalists most attentive *to Pralle*, to her home, and then putting them on the phone with Wuornos.

Although Pralle "meant well," her own need to talk, mainly about herself, and about her love for both Jesus and Wuornos, posed grave dangers to the defense. For example, the telephone calls could be taped or the prosecution could read "all about it" in newspapers and magazines. At first, Pralle insisted that Wuornos was a "good" person and that she couldn't have killed in cold blood; Pralle also said she expected Jesus to perform a miracle. Once Wuornos was sentenced to death, Pralle publicly supported Wuornos's desire to die and to "go home to Jesus."

Pralle and Wuornos engaged in a *folie a deux*, a "you and me, babe, against the world," which both women must

113

have experienced as supportive, even thrilling, given the intense media attention being focused on them. (Like Wuornos, Pralle was also abandoned by her biological mother and had seriously attempted suicide.) However, the fact that a "traditional" woman stood up for Wuornos is as moving as it is bizarre.

Wuornos also had the (questionable) support of Steven Glazer, Pralle's own lawyer, who helped Wuornos achieve four more death sentences, and who, as previously noted, charged the media for Death Row interviews with his client, disbursing the money to Wuornos, Pralle, and to himself.[126]

Jury deliberation in the Wuornos case was surprisingly brief: on January 30, 1992, her jury of five men and seven women needed only one hour and 31 minutes to find her guilty, and only one hour and 48 minutes to recommend the death penalty. (In Ted Bundy's case, the jury took seven hours to find him guilty and seven and a half hours to sentence him to death.) On January 31, 1992, Judge Blount, who could have overridden the jury's recommendation, ordered that Wuornos die in the electric chair for the murder of 51-year-old ex-convict Richard Mallory. She was immediately taken to Death Row at the Broward County Correctional Facility for Women.

If the state of Florida could, it would electrocute Wuornos once for each man she's accused of killing. (She has so far been sentenced to death five times.) But what are Wuornos's true crimes?

Wuornos stands accused of being a man-hating lesbian, a description that could not endear her to the sheriffs, wardens, lawyers, judges, or jurors in an area of Florida where the local abortion clinic was burned right down to the ground not once, but twice in the years between 1989 and 1991; where crosses have been burned with alarming regularity on the lawns of African-American families; and where residents were responsible for the third largest individual, out-of-state contribution to David Dukes's most recent gubernatorial campaign. Someone like Wuornos has little support in the state known as the "Buckle of the Death Sentence Belt."

Is Wuornos guilty of being a prostitute? Or is she guilty of not having killed herself—the way all "good" sexual abuse victims and prostituted women are supposed to do? Or—shades of "Thelma and Louise" and the backlash against clemency for battered women who kill in self-defense—is Wuornos guilty of daring to defend herself in a violent struggle with a man and, by example, encouraging other prostitutes (and non-prostitutes) to do likewise?

A Woman's Right To Self-Defense

As previously noted, in the nineteenth and twentieth centuries, both prostituted and non-prostituted women, and slaves, sometimes injured and killed violent male non-intimates in self-defense.[127] From 1970 to 1992, both prostituted and non-prostituted women have charged rape and battery or attempted rape and battery and claimed they killed in self-defense.[128] Only a handful have been believed.

In the early 1970s, grass-roots feminists, civil rights activists, the Center for Constitutional Rights, and the Southern Poverty Law Center focused on three cases in which women of color had killed violent male non-intimates in self-defense. I am referring to the cases of Yvonne Wanrow,[129] Joan Little,[130] and Inez Garcia.[131]

Joan Little was a black woman who killed a white jail guard who attempted to rape her in the jail cell in which she was incarcerated for a burglary conviction. She was represented by Morris Dees and acquitted in 1975. Inez Garcia was raped, and she shot the man who held her down later that same day. She was convicted, but her conviction was overturned on appeal.

At this time, I will discuss only the decision of *State v. Wanrow*,[132] in which the Supreme Court of Washington affirmed the reversal of the conviction of Yvonne Wanrow for second-degree murder and first-degree assault with a deadly weapon.[133]

The facts of *Wanrow* were as follows: On the afternoon of August 11, 1972, Yvonne Wanrow, a Colville Indian woman who was a single mother and an artist, left her two children at the home of her friend, Ms. Hooper. After playing in the neighborhood, Ms. Wanrow's son returned to Ms. Hooper's home and told her that a man had tried to pull him off his bicycle and drag him into a house. A few months prior to this incident, Ms. Hooper's seven-year-old daughter had suffered from a venereal disease, contracted after being molested by a man whose identity she would not reveal to her mother. A few minutes after Ms. Wanrow's son told his story to Ms. Hooper, the decedent, William Wesler, appeared at Ms. Hooper's house and stated through the door, "I didn't touch the kid, I didn't touch the kid."[134] At that moment, Ms. Hooper's daughter, seeing Wesler at the door, identified Wesler as the man who had molested her. Ms. Hooper's landlord then informed her that Wesler, a six-foot-two-inch white man who had been committed to an institution for the mentally ill, had molested another child who had previously lived in the same house.[135] Ms. Hooper immediately summoned the police, who arrived shortly thereafter and advised Ms. Hooper to wait until Monday to get a warrant for Wesler's arrest.

That evening, Ms. Hooper called Ms. Wanrow, related the incident, and asked her to spend the night. Ms. Wanrow arrived sometime after 6 p.m. with a pistol in her handbag. Still afraid to stay alone, Ms. Hooper and Ms. Wanrow called Ms. Wanrow's sister and brother-in-law, Angie and Chuck Mitchell, who agreed to spend the night. At approximately 5 a.m., Chuck Mitchell, without informing the women, went to Wesler's home with a baseball bat and accused Wesler of molesting children. Wesler then suggested they all discuss the incident, and together with a third man, Wesler and Mitchell returned to Ms. Hooper's home to straighten out the problem. Wesler, however, was the only man to enter the house.

Wesler, then visibly intoxicated, entered Ms. Hooper's home and refused to leave when asked to do so. Confusion and shouting followed, and a young child—one of eight then staying at the house—awoke crying. Testimony indicated that Wesler approached the child, stating, "My what a cute little boy," and Ms. Hooper began screaming for Wesler to get out.[136] Wanrow, five-foot-four-inch with a broken leg and using a crutch, went to the door to ask Mitchell for help. When Ms. Wanrow turned around, Wesler was standing directly behind her. Startled by her situation, Ms. Wanrow testified as to having shot Wesler in what amounted to a reflex action.

At trial, Ms. Wanrow argued that she had acted in self-defense. The jury was instructed that in evaluating the gravity of the danger to Ms. Wanrow, the jury was to consider only those acts and circumstances occurring "at or immediately before the killing...."[137] Ms. Wanrow was convicted of second-degree murder and first-degree assault with a deadly weapon.[138]

In affirming the reversal of Ms. Wanrow's conviction, the Supreme Court of Washington held that the trial court had erred in limiting the jury instruction on self-defense.[139] Instead, the jury should have been instructed to evaluate the justification of self-defense "in light of *all* the facts and circumstances known to [Ms. Wanrow], including those known substantially before the killing."[140] The court stated that the jury should have been instructed to consider Ms. Wanrow's knowledge of Wesler's reputation for aggressive behavior, despite the fact that Wesler's reputation was based on events which had occurred over a period of years and that Ms. Wanrow had received this information several hours before the incident. This information would aid in the "critical determination of the 'degree of force which...a reasonable person in the same situation...seeing what (s)he sees and knowing what (s)he knows, then would believe to be necessary'."[141]

In addition, the court held that Ms. Wanrow's actions were to be judged against her own "subjective impressions [of danger] and not those which a detached jury might determine to be objectively reasonable."[142] In recognizing the special circumstances which often accompany a woman's assertion of self-defense, the court acknowledged that "women suffer from a conspicuous lack of access to training in and the means of developing those skills necessary to effectively repel a male assailant without resorting to the use of deadly weapons."[143] With respect to the delivery of jury instructions, the court cautioned that the persistent use of the masculine gender leaves the jury with the impression the objective standard to be applied is that applicable to an altercation between two men. The impression created—that a five-foot four-inch woman with a cast on her leg and using a crutch must, under the law, somehow repel an assault by a six-foot two-inch intoxicated man without employing weapons in her defense, unless the jury finds her determination of the degree of danger to be objectively reasonable—constitutes a separate and distinct misstatement of the law and, in the context of this case, violates the respondent's right to equal protection of the law. [Ms. Wanrow] was entitled to have the jury consider her actions in the light of her own perceptions of the situation, including those perceptions which were the product of our nation's 'long and unfortunate history of sex discrimination.' Until such time as the effects of that history are eradicated, care must be taken to assure that our self-defense instructions afford women the right to have their conduct judged in light of the individual physical handicaps which are the product of sex discrimination. To fail to do so is to deny the right of the individual woman involved to trial by the same rules which are applicable to male defendants.[144]

Since the *Wanrow* decision, a number of articles on feminist jurisprudence have appeared, attempting to further clarify the circumstances under which a *reasonable woman* can argue self-defense, especially after she has been sexually and physically assaulted, or has killed to avoid being assaulted or killed.[145] In 1978, Elizabeth Schneider, who was Wanrow's lawyer in the successful appeal to the Washington Supreme Court, and co-author Susan Jordan, commented on the Wanrow case, noting that the [c]ircumstances under which women are forced to defend themselves [are] entirely different from those which cause men to commit homicides, [and] the woman's state of mind is different as well. Presenting the individual woman's perspective in the trial means educating the judge and jury about the incidence and severity of the problems of rape, wife-assault, and child abuse and molestation.... It also means educating them about the lack of judicial and social alternatives available to women in these situations and combating specific myths, for example, that a woman who kills a man is insane or that women enjoy rape.

State v. Wanrow is an example of successful implementation of this strategy.

In a landmark decision, [the *Wanrow* court]...acknowledged the threat to equal protection inherent in the failure to include a woman's perspective in the law of self-defense....[146]

According to Schneider and Jordan, despite the fact that women are targets for male violence, and tend to be shorter and to weigh less than men, women are not socialized to defend themselves, generally have no experience of combat, tackle sports, or street fighting, and are actually dissuaded from using violence against men as a cultural imperative.[147] Thus, at this point in history, when women perceive themselves to be in mortal danger, perhaps they should be/are entitled to use weapons as the only way to exert comparable force against a male assailant.

In 1982, Catharine Mackinnon also commented on Wanrow. She wrote:

> Wanrow is an exceptional woman because she fought back. She, therefore, receives the benefit of the history of all women who have not, presumably because they were disabled from doing so. It seems that you have to behave more like a man to get the benefit of being considered as a woman.... *Wanrow*, in this light, is not about fighting back, although that is what its result supports. It is more as if the state will help keep women from being walked on so long as we struggle while down, but it may not support us if we stand up.[148]

Mackinnon does not think the Washington State Supreme Court went far enough in establishing a "subjective" standard for a reasonable woman's right to self-defense. Mackinnon concludes that

> The reasonable woman's subjectivity is equivalent to women's point of view under conditions of sex discrimination. The *Wanrow* court thus uses a subjective test to place the jury in the defendant's immediate surroundings but goes well beyond traditional notions of subjectivity (without becoming objective) in attributing to her a consciousness for acting that first sets her in the concrete historical context of gender and then attributes the meaning of that context to her mentality and physicality.[149]

Since the *Wanrow* decision, many women have alleged rape self-defense; few have been believed (e.g., *Shirley Mae Thomas v. State*, 578 South Western Reporter, 2nd Series

1975 (Texas); *Commonwealth v. Lamrini* 467 N.E. 2nd 95
1984 Mass 1984; *Commonwealth v. Carbone*, 574 Atlantic
Reporter, 2nd Series Pa. 1990). An increasing number of articles on feminist jurisprudence have also tried to clarify, further, the circumstances under which a *reasonable woman* can
argue rape/battery self-defense.[150]

Burning questions remain. They include: Does a woman
have the right to kill to prevent herself from being raped? In
the past, courts have refused to impose the death penalty on
rape[151] or to hold that forced sex constitutes "great bodily
injury" to trigger penalty enhancement[152]—despite the fact
that the consequences of rape are often life-long and extremely debilitating. If a woman only has the right to use whatever
force, *short of homicide*, necessary to prevent rape, how can
she know exactly how much or how little force to employ to
make her escape? *How does a woman know that a rapist will
stop at rape?* Does a woman have the same right to "heat-of-
passion" and rage to protect her bodily integrity and "honor"
that men do? Does a man's Fourteenth Amendment right to
use deadly force to prevent burglary or other invasions of his
home and castle cover a woman's right to prevent any
unwanted invasion of her body? Is a woman's "right to equality" a right to have inequality taken into account?

From about 1967 on, in addition to fighting for wom-
en's right to abortion and to equal pay for equal work, grass-
roots feminists focused on the sexual objectification of
women, and on issues of sexual violence toward women, such
as stranger-rape and sexual harassment on the job and on the
street. Only after a decade were feminist activists able to
expand their focus to include marital rape, date rape, domestic battery, and incest. During the 1980s, it became clear (to
feminists working in the area) that most prostituted women
were also incest victims, that many battered wives were treated as if they were their husbands' or boyfriends' prostitutes,

that both wife-batterers and serial killers of women were addicted to pornography, and that *all* women, whether they were prostitutes (the so-called "bad girls") or non-prostitutes (the so-called "good girls"), who dared to kill in self-defense were treated as if they were prostitutes, i.e., demon terrorists from hell who deserved no mercy.

As yet, no radical feminist equivalent to the Center for Constitutional Rights or the Southern Poverty Law Center exists, nor does even one overarching graduate/medical/law school program committed to centralizing, summarizing, and updating the relevant research and training of expert witnesses in this area. The media often decides which cases the nation will follow, not feminists, who are increasingly without resources, exhausted, and under seige.

The Battered Woman's Syndrome Defense was developed by feminists to help explain to juries how, for example, a woman could stay with a batterer, refuse to report him, and then one day kill him *when he is sleeping*—and claim "self-defense." However, this approach is highly controversial among feminists.[153] Critics say: If a woman defends herself in order to save her life, why view (or explain) female self-defense as a form of "diminished capacity," as "temporary insanity," or as "post-traumatic stress syndrome"? Either the woman's life was being threatened—or not; either, as a reasonable women, she believed her life to be in danger and she acted in self-defense—or she didn't. Why view a woman's exercise of a legal right as a psychiatric disability?[154] Perhaps the (battered) woman who finally kills to escape being tortured has experienced a sudden "flight into mental health," and should not be viewed as psychologically "disabled" for having stood up for herself.

Although I will not go into this here, it is my understanding that the Battered Woman's Syndrome Defense does not necessarily suggest a psychiatric disability—although the

Defense is often perceived as such. Theorists, such as Schneider, Jordan, Walker, and others, have suggested that this defense is meant to educate the jury about how widespread anti-woman domestic and sexual violence is and about what the *normal* human (female) response to prolonged violence is.[155]

Given what we now know about how often prostituted women are raped, gang-raped, beaten, robbed, tortured, and killed, Wuornos's claim that she killed six out of hundreds or thousands of violent johns, in self-defense, is plausible. Wuornos's claim certainly merited far more thought and consideration than the deliberate neglect it received from those who heard and tried her case.

Latest Developments

As disappointed as I was in Jenkins's defense of Wuornos, Jenkins and co-counsel Billy Nolas and William Miller look radiantly efficient compared to her next and current lawyer, Steven Glazer of Gainesville. Glazer, a civil lawyer, was originally recommended by Trish Jenkins not as a defense attorney, but to handle Wuornos's adoption by Pralle.[156]

I phoned Glazer for the first time on March 1, 1992. He told me he was not interested in having me or any other pro bono expert testify for the defense in upcoming trials two through six, nor was he interested in handling Wuornos's appeal of the Mallory conviction or in a future campaign for clemency. Glazer said he was only interested in how much money I was willing to pay for the right to interview Wuornos on Death Row, that his client had empowered him to do this and no more. Glazer told me that Dolores Kennedy, together with Robert Nolin, who have since published *On A Killing Day* (and who ultimately never got to interview Wuornos), had offered $10,000 cash up front with an additional percentage of the paperback monies.[157]

Glazer further told me that because he saw a "career" for himself in attracting criminals with stories to sell, his association with Wuornos would definitely be a "good advertisement." He added that he needed the money the media was willing to pay to interview Wuornos in order to fund his fight against the state of Florida if and when, despite the recent Supreme Court ruling overturning New York's Son-of-Sam law,[158] Florida officials tried to interfere with Wuornos's ability to profit from her crimes and to assist her in her criminal cases as best he could. Also, Glazer pointed out, money was needed to pay for Arlene Pralle's visits to Death Row and to save Pralle's heavily mortgaged horse-farm.[159]

When I called Glazer a "pimp," he hung up on me and instructed Wuornos to cease communicating with me—which she did from mid-March to mid-June, 1992 and again from mid-August to October, 1992.[160]

In March of 1992, shortly after our conversation, Glazer had Wuornos plead "no contest" in Marion County in three additional trials. In open court, Glazer likened himself to the "Dr. Jack Kevorkian of the legal world," and asked Judge Thomas Sawaya to "assist him in helping his client to commit suicide."[161] (What next? A lawyer who offers to pull the switch? A lawyer who scalps tickets for front-row seats in the execution chamber?) Wuornos was sentenced to death three more times.

Wuornos is confined to a cage on Death Row by a legal order; I'm confined at home, often in bed, by Chronic Fatigue Immune Dysfunction Syndrome. I have imaginary conversations with her almost every day.

Lee: you hit the ground running before either Thelma or Louise came to town. You're the real star of that movie; it's about you, about what you've done, about what to do, when men, truckers for example, or police officers in unmarked

124

cars: you know, ordinary married men, the mainstay of your profession, start making those sounds and faces at women, any women, it's nothing personal, some women even take it as a compliment, and with one hand on the wheel, the other somewhere out of sight, say: "Wanna sit on my face, suck my cock, let me fuck you in the ass," as they follow the teen-age hitchhiker, or the mother of teen-agers, it makes no difference: whether the hitch-hiker's own car has broken down, or whether she's just been dumped on the highway by her boyfriend for refusing to put out, or whether she's just been raped by the previous man-in-a-moving-vehicle, or whether she's just out riding to clear her mind. There's no law against trying, is there?

You probably don't know what I'm talking about; you were behind bars when Thelma and Louise were on the lam.

Talk about women who run with the wolves! You've navigated North America's vast, frozen tundra, with a craftiness, a cunning, a scavenging genius, without which neither wild life nor prostitutes could survive: not for a day, not for an hour.

Often, you've been shown "grinning like a damn fool" as if you're at the Mad Hatter's tea party with a lampshade on your head. You're the Queen, yelling "off with his head." And you're smiling, as they say, "inappropriately." You know: that smile women smile when we're embarrassed by insults, and scared: as if our compliance, our willingness to act as if we're not in danger, will keep us safe. You've had lots of practice in this area.

I visited Wuornos in July of 1992.

"Far out, man" she said. "You're from the Women's Lib aren't you? Tell the women out there that I'm innocent. Tell them that men hate our guts. I was raped and I defended myself. It was self-defense. I could not stop hustling just because some asshole was going around Florida raping and killing women. I still had to hustle."

Her voice was Joplin-husky and surprisingly sweet, even girlish. (Did I expect her to sound like a man?) Well, honey, that's a real hefty swagger she wore on TV, and the way she tossed her hair around: most women do it out of nervousness; she seemed to do it out of defiance, to intimidate: the way male lions toss their manes.

She said that jail didn't "bother" her, that she could "take it," that the daily verbal abuse was nothing: "Hey, whore, show us some tits 'n' puss"; "Here's a little present just from us guys: our come, all nice and wet in this envelope, with your name on it"; "We'll put you in solitary forever if you do any weird lesbian shit in here: bark at the moon, bitch, if you don't like it"; "I'm going to enjoy watching you fry, real nice and slowly, once for each guy you killed."

The heartlessness of these words would kill me. My life has rendered me unfit to survive her jail cell; her life has groomed her to do so.

"I need you guys real bad," she answered. "The public defender has 47 other capital cases and no time for me. I'll pay you back if you get me a lawyer who has time for me. I'll sell my life story for 30 million dollars and I'll set up a foundation for abused women. Hey, man: I'm going through living hell for defending myself."

And then, with wonderment, she said: "I can't believe there are women out there rooting for me!"

Well, not so fast. Yes, many women, actually a surprising number, have said: "It's about time women started shooting back," and "Good for her. Those men must have done something to provoke her: they're johns, they deserved it." Some feminists (and anti-death penalty advocates) have urged me to do everything I can for her. But most women, including feminists and lesbians, see her as too unsympathetic a victim to bother with: unstable, uncooperative, a loser, a real pain-in-the-ass, and just plain nuts.

Know: that I don't romanticize her. How could I? She's as conventional as most (abused) women are. For example: she's quite the "Golly gee whizz" kind of "good ol' gal," when she talks about how some of her best friends are johns, and about how she believes in Jesus, always did, and that He's coming too. She "enjoyed" the sex-for-money with men, she's proud she was able to "please" her dates/customers/johns. She's an outlaw by default, not by choice.

The women who kill violent men are *all* "good girls" who've bought into the very system that I dream of destroying. When they realize they've been tricked (talk about "tricks"!), had, taken, left for dead, and that no one will help them, they're invisible anyway, maybe that's when they kill the man who's been breaking their bones for years; the one hundredth john who's taking his knife out and threatening to cut their face/breasts/anus/vagina; the man who's just walked out with custody of their kids, the deed to their home, and a new wife on his arm.

As THE (so-called) FIRST FEMALE SERIAL KILLER, she's made headlines, not for what has been done to her, but for what she's *done*. Her bullets shattered the silence about violence against prostituted women, about women fighting back: and about what happens to them when they do.

No small feat.

I doubt she was avenging the billions, no trillions, of other women who were killed at birth, or abandoned, starved, beaten, genitally mutilated, sold into marriage, pornography, or prostitution, raped, impregnated, sterilized, impoverished, all against their will, or killed: simply *because they were women*, or *prostituted* women, or *lesbians*.

But even if I thought she'd led the equivalent of a slave-revolt, planned a raid on Harper's Ferry, left the Massa's House in flames behind her, this is not something most women can do. Our fear of certain, further, punishment is too great.

For example, unlike her, I didn't buy a gun. Instead, I clipped and filed all the grisly notices of our dead: I mean to have them engraved on a vast memorial tombstone or stitched into a quilt, like the parents of murdered children do. I'm angry, don't think I'm not, but I just can't go out and kill someone. I'm a "girl." We turn our terror and our anger against ourselves, not against others.

So here's what's troubling me. How could she, a "nobody," have summoned up enough grit and righteous rage to save her own life? (Is that it, she had nothing to lose, she knew no one would save her but herself, so she did that—and got arrested for saving her own life?)

Wuornos is led into the room by two guards. She is unsteady on her feet, a bit ungainly, not that tall.

I remember how she looked when she was first arrested. Spirited, defiant, drunk, the swagger and the smirk: all gone, all gaunt, not an ounce of flesh on her bones. She is more ghost than human.

Wuornos's blond hair is pale, and pulled back into a thin pony tail. Her face is taut, her features bony, inexpressive: no energy to waste on "expressiveness." Survival in prison demands that she contract everything: movements, even dreams, in order to conserve energy, call as little attention to herself as possible.

She has great dignity. She has come from some truly far-away place to meet me, she is jerky in her motions, but gamely, she's trying to smile. As if it's a social occasion. We hug hello: briefly, carefully.

I'm always amazed—although I shouldn't be—when those with no formal education, no money, no health, no friends in high places, and nothing to hope for, absolutely rise to the occasion of their 15 minutes of fame: and with extraordinary eloquence and grace. Mary Beth Whitehead, in the Baby M case, for example, was almost regal in how she handled both the media and our little demonstrations outside the courthouse. Whitehead was well-spoken and, of course, loved the opportunity to "shine." No crime, by the way.

Wuornos has been in jail for two years now, a lot of the time in isolation. She says she was "railroaded" because she's a prostitute and "expendable," and they'd just "bend, twist, distort" any new evidence, so she'd rather die and "go home to Jesus" than keep living (if that's the word for what you do on Death Row). "It's all over" she says. Wuornos doesn't want to go to Chatahoochie ("I'm not crazy"), and she doesn't want to stay on Death Row, so she's decided to die.

You don't have to be crazy to come to this decision.

Wuornos is emphatic. Despite what she's written: that she wants me to find her a lawyer, and a private investigator, and to reassemble the team of pro bono experts I'd gathered for her first trial, she's changed her mind again. She grows more animated, angry, and, trigger-finger pointed, orders me to "Forget it. All I want you to do is help me expose the corruption, the crooked cops, the media deals, the capital gains off a capital crime. Tell the world what's going on. That's all. I'm not concerned about any more trials."

In a not-yet-released 1993 BBC documentary *Aileen Carol Wuornos: The Selling of a Serial Killer*, Wuornos describes Arlene Pralle, the woman who adopted her before the first trial and Steve Glazer, the lawyer who performed the adoption and who helped Wuornos plead "no contest" or "guilty" in trials two, three, four and five, as "the money-hungry people. That's their main purpose—money and to see me die. Steve and Arlene are doing a lot of lying in the media. Their motive was just to make money. I'll [expose them] later, just before I go [die].... They convinced and connived me not to contest. Arlene started it and Steve just fell in. Arlene told me 'I just can't take it, all these trials, you're killing your new adoptive mother.... [In a death penalty state] why not go for it and be home with Jesus?' They're not on my side, they're not very lawyerly or motherly, but it's too late."

On camera, Glazer is shown taking money from BBC film director Nick Broomfield for the right to interview Wuornos, Arlene, and himself; Broomfield says that Glazer is talking about "selling film rights to Wuornos's execution to the highest bidder."

How can someone like Wuornos keep fighting back? She held on, as best she could, did her best, actually acquitted herself nobly in the first trial, and it didn't matter, nothing mattered, the "scumbags of America," as she called the jury, convicted her anyway.

I ask her if anyone ever helped her when she was a child, sleeping in abandoned cars and living on the street, or later on. She says: "I raised myself. I did a pretty good job. I taught myself my own handwriting, and I studied theology, psychology, books on self-enhancement. I taught myself how to draw. I have been through battles out there raising myself. I'm like a Marine, you can't hurt me. If you hurt me, I can wipe it out of my mind and keep on truckin'. I took every day on a day-by-day basis. I never let things dwell inside me to damage my pride because I knew what that felt like when I was young..."

A child is being beaten...how to intervene? What to do when no one ever intervened and now it's much too late, the damage is done, the child is a woman, and the woman only knows that she must sell (her body, and now her life-story, her death), in order to live and to be of value. By now, she hates having to sell, hates *not* being able to sell, hates the seller, hates the buyer; she's weary, cynical, heartbroken, used up, and is, by now, simply not capable (if she ever was) of doing something: anything, that will turn out right for her.

Wuornos has been waiting, wanting, trying to die for a long time. Now, she means to finish what the men, and We, the People, have started. Her destruction.

In late October and early November, 1992, Glazer called and asked me to find a competent lawyer for Wuornos. He admitted that although he "meant well" and would "do anything to help Lee," he might not have done "right" by his client, and that he had a heart condition that required surgery.

Christopher Quarles, of the Marion County Public Defender's Office, filed the state-level appeal of Wuornos's first conviction in October, 1992. (This appeal was re-filed in January of 1993.) Steven Glazer, however, never filed notice that he or his client wished to appeal the second, third, and fourth death sentences. Chief Assistant State Attorney Ric Ridgway, who prosecuted Wuornos, said that Glazer's failure to file the appeals could lead Wuornos to claim Glazer was "ineffective."

Ridgway said that he doesn't know whether Wuornos wants to appeal, but that her counsel inadvertently has prevented her from exercising that right.

"Glazer, evidently, was operating under the impression that this court would appoint the public defender's office to handle the appeal," Ridgway wrote in his motion to force Glazer to appeal.

Glazer said he got a phone call from Tallahassee about a month ago asking for Wuornos's paperwork.

"[Lee] doesn't want to appeal, but she doesn't have a choice," Glazer said. "I told the judge my client has ordered me not to appeal, that's why the judge appointed the public defender because it seems like I have a natural conflict."[162]

In November of 1992, just after asking for my help in obtaining another lawyer, Glazer pled Wuornos "guilty" in the fifth case in Dixie County—and renegotiated (or "upgraded") her contract with Hollywood producer Giroux.[163]

From the start, people consistently asked me if Wuornos was "crazy." (Never if she was "guilty"; most were convinced she was.) It probably wouldn't be hard to diagnose Wuornos as a "borderline" or "multiple" or "addictive" personality. But, according to most recent studies, such diagnoses are simply ways of *stigmatizing* Wuornos for the consequences of being an incest, child abuse, and serial rape victim.[164]

Everyone in Wuornos's life—her family of origin, her childhood neighbors, her teachers, the home for unwed mothers, the Michigan juvenile and Florida adult correctional facilities, her lesbian lover, and the entire cast of "serial killer" characters: the prosecution, the defense, the private lawyers, the judges, the juries, the investigating police officers, Hollywood and the media, even We, the People—conspired, through acts of commission, omission, indifference, and negligence, to deprive Wuornos of the most minimal justice.

NOTES

1. See Jean Dubail, "Police Seek Clues Along Trail of 8 Deaths," *Orlando Sentinel*, Dec. 9, 1990, at B1; Tom Lyons, "Two Sets of North Florida Killings Differ Markedly," *Gainesville Sun*, Dec. 7, 1990, at 1A; Marion "Police Fear Someone's Stalking, Killing Middle-Aged Men," *Orlando Sentinel*, Dec. 1, 1990, at D9; Rick Tonyan, "Voluisa Police Hunt for 2 Linked to Killings," *Orlando Sentinel*, Dec. 19, 1990, at D3.

2. See Elizabeth Rapaport, "Some Questions About Gender and the Death Penalty," 20 *Golden Gate U. L. Rev.* 501 (1990); Victor Steib, "Death Penalty for Female Offenders," 58 *Cinn. L. Rev.* 845 (1990); Victor L. Streib

and Lynn Sametz, "Executing Female Juveniles," 22 *Conn. L.. Rev.* 3 (1989); Victor L. Streib, "American Executions of Female Offenders: A Preliminary Inventory of Names, Dates, and Other Information" (prepared for distribution to research colleagues) (1988) (on file with author); Victor L. Streib, "Capital Punishment for Female Offenders: Present Female Death Row Inmates and Death Sentences and Executions of Female Offenders" (May 1, 1991) (on file with author).

3. See Freda Adler, *Sisters In Crime: The Rise of the New Female Criminal* (1975); Lowell Cauffiel, *Forever and Five Days* (1992); Ann Jones, *Women Who Kill* (1981); Beverly Lowry, *Crossed Over* (1992); Rita J. Simon and Jean Landis, *The Crimes Women Commit* (1991); Charlene Snow, *Women in Prison* (1981); William Wilbanks, *Female Homicide Offenders in the U.S.* ( ); Coramae R. Mann, "Women Who Kill Someone They Don't Really Know," Paper presented at American Sociological Association Meeting (1987); Coramae R. Mann, "Black Women Who Kill," in *Violence in the Black Family*, 157-86 (Robert L. Hampton ed., 1987); William Wilbanks, "Murdered Women and Women Who Murder: A Critique of the Literature," in *Judge, Lawyer, Victim, Thief: Women, Gender Roles, and Criminal Justice*, 157 (Nicole H. Ratter and Elizabeth A. Stanko eds., 1982); Angela Browne and Kirk R. Williams, "Exploring the Effect of Resource Availability and the Likelihood of Female-Perpetrated Homicides," 23 *Law & Society* 75 (1989); Coramae R. Mann, "Black Female Homicide in the United States," 5 *J. Interpersonal Violence* 176 (1990); Carol Smart, "The New Female Criminal: Reality or Myth?", 19 *Brit. J. Criminology* 50 (1979).

4. See Angela Browne, *When Battered Women Kill* (1987); Cynthia K. Gillespie, *Justifiable Homicide* (1989)(addressing legal status of abused women in the United States); Jonathan Goodman, *Thirteen Classic True Crime Stories*

(1990); Ann Jones, *Everyday Death: The Case of Bernadette Powell* (1985); Susan Schechter, *Women and Male Violence* (1982); Jocelynne Scutt, *Even in the Best of Homes: Violence in the Family* (1983); Snow, supra note 3; Lenore E. Walker, *Terrifying Love: Why Battered Women Kill and How Society Responds* (1989); Lenore E. Walker, *The Battered Woman* (1979); Wilbanks, supra note 3; Nancy Jurik and Russ Winn, "Gender and Homicide: A Comparison of Men and Women Who Kill," *5 Violence & Victims* 229 (1990).

5. See Phyllis Chesler, *Women and Madness* (1972, 1989); Phyllis Chesler, "The Amazon Legacy: An Interpretive Essay," in *Wonder Woman* (1972) (citing early works of Hesiod, 720 B.C.; Homer, 820 B.C.; Plutarch, A.D. 80; Tacitus, A.D. 100; Thuydides, 430 B.C.; Virgil, 40 B.C.). Female warriors and killers have been the subject of literature dating back to the early nineteenth century: Johann J. Bachofen, *Myth, Religion, and Mother Right* (Ralph Manheim trans., 1967)(first published in three volumes in Switzerland in the nineteenth century); Robert Briffault, *The Mothers* (1963)(first published in 1927); Sir Richard Francis Burton, *A Mission to Gelele, King of Dahome* (1966)(first published in 1864); Elizabeth G. Davis, *The First Sex* (1971); Helen Diner, *Mothers and Amazons: The First Feminine History of Culture* (John Philip Lundin trans., 1973)(first published in Austria in the 1930s); Edward Gibbon, *The Decline and Fall of the Roman Empire: and other selected writings* (J.B. Bury ed., 1896); Robert Graves, *The White Goddess: A Historical Grammar of Poetic Myth* (1948); Jane E. Harrison, *Prolegomena to the Study of Greek Religion* (1903); Charles G. Jung and Caroly Kerenyi, *Essays on a Science of Mythology: The Myth of the Divine Child and the Divine Maiden* (R.F.C. Hull trans., 1949); Caroly Kerenyi, *Eleusis: Archetypal Image of Mother and Daughter* (Ralph Manheim trans., 1967); Lewis H. Morgan, *Ancient Society* (1978); Margaret A. Murray, *The Splendor That Was Egypt* (1963); Erich

Neumann, *The Great Mother* (1955); Regine Pernoud, *Joan of Arc by Herself and Her Witnesses* (Edward Hyams trans., 1964); Phillip E. Slater, *The Glory of Hera: Greek Mythology and the Greek Family* (1971). The following are more recent sources that have been helpful on the subject: Antonia Fraser, *The Warrior Queens: The Legends and the Lives of the Women Who Have Led Their Nations in War* (1989); Abby W. Kleinbaum, *The War Against the Amazons* (1983); Victoria Sackville-West, *Saint Joan of Arc* (1991); Jessica A. Salmonson, *The Encyclopedia of Amazons: Women Warriors from Antiquity to the Modern Era* (1991).

6. See, e.g., Kathleen Barry, *Susan B. Anthony: A Biography of a Singular Feminist*, 3 (1988) (discussing 1871 case of prostitute Laura Fair, who killed local dignitary in self-defense); Timothy Gilfoyle, *City of Eros: NYC Prostitution and The Commercialization of Sex 1790-1920* (1992); Jones, supra note 3, at 147-52 (discussing 1843 case of prostitute Amelia Norman, 1855 case of Mary Moriarty, 1865 case of Mary Harris, and 1872 case of Fanny Windley); Melton A. McLaurin, *Celia A Slave* (1991) (discussing case of sexually abused Missouri slave, Celia, who killed her master).

7. See U.S. Dept. of Justice, *Sourcebook of Criminal Justice Statistics*, Table 4.19 (Kathleen Maguire and Timothy Flalagar eds., 1990); Ann W. Burgess et al., "Serial Rapists and Their Victims: Reenactment and Repetition," *Annals N.Y. Acad. Sci.* (1987); Ann W. Burgess, "Murderers Who Rape and Mutilate," 1 *J. Interpersonal Violence* 273 (1986).

8. See, e.g., Deborah Cameron and Elizabeth Frazer, *The Lust to Kill* (1987); Jane Caputi, *The Age of Sex Crime* (1987); Eric W. Hickey, *Serial Murderers and Their Victims* (1991); Louise Malette et al. eds., (1991) *The Montreal Massacre*; Jill Radford and Diana Russell eds., (1992) *Femicide: The Politics of Women Killing*; Colin Wilson, *Written in Blood:*

The Criminal Mind and Method (1989); Steven J. Michaud and Hugh Aynesworth, *The Only Living Witness: A True Account of Homicidal Insanity* (1983); Tim Cahill, *Buried Dreams: Inside The Mind of a Serial Killer* (1986); Art Crockett, *Serial Murderers* (1990); Robert Graysmith, *Zodiac* (1986); Robert Graysmith, *The Sleeping Lady: The Trailside Murder Above the Golden Gate* (1991); Clifford L. Linedecker, *The Man Who Killed Boys: A True Story of Mass Murder in a Chicago Suburb* (1980); Clifford L. Linedecker, *Night Stalker* (1991); Ann Rule, *The I-5 Killer* (1984); Ann Rule, *The Stranger Beside Me* (1981); Harold Schechter, *Deviant: The Shocking Story of Ed Gein, the Original "Psycho"* (1989); Ted Schwartz, *The Hillside Strangler: A Murderer's Mind* (1982); Carlton Smith and Thomas Guillen, *The Search for the Green River Killer* (1991); Maury Terry, *The Ultimate Evil* (1987).

9. See Browne, supra note 4; Phyllis Chesler, *Mothers on Trial: The Battle for Children and Custody*, 293-96 (1986, 1991); Gillespie, supra note 4, at 1-31; Jones, supra note 3, at 320; Jurik and Winn, supra note 4, at 236; Schechter, supra note 4, at 170-74; Walker, *Terrifying Love*, supra note 4, at 12; Walker, *Battered Woman*, supra note 4; Lynne A. Foster et al., "Factors Present When Battered Women Kill," 10 *Issues in Mental Health Nursing* 273 (1989).

10. See Chesler, *Mothers on Trial*, supra note 9, at 295-96; Florida Supreme Court Gender Bias Study Commission, Gender Bias in Criminal Justice 170 (Mar. 1990) [hereinafter Gender Bias Rep.]. See Margaret A. Baldwin, "Split at the Root: Prostitution and Feminist Discourses of Law Reform," *Yale J.L. & Feminisim* (1993).

11. See Kentucky Task Force on Gender Fairness in the Courts 41 (Jan. 13, 1992). "In Kentucky, women accounted for only eighteen percent of the total arrests in 1990. Of those, only 2.9% were arrested for violent crime." Id.; Chesler, *Mothers on Trial*, supra note 9; Jones, supra note 3, at 12,

13; Ann Stanton, *When Mothers Go To Jail* (1980); Dorothy Zeitz, *Women Who Embezzle or Defraud: A Study of Convicted Felons* (1983); Charlene Snow, "Women Who Go to Jail," *Clearinghouse Review* (1981).

12. See Chesler, *Mothers on Trial*, supra note 9, at 291. For more in-depth discussion of prostitution and sexual and pyschological exploitation, see Ann Snitow et al., *Powers of Desire: The Politics of Sexuality* 419-39 (1983); Kathleen Barry, *Female Sexual Slavery* (1979); Kathleen Barry et al., *International Feminism: Networking Against Female Sexual Slavery: Report of the Global Feminist Workshop to Organize Against Traffic in Women in Rotterdam, the Netherlands April 6-15, 1983* (1984); Arlene Carmen and Howard Moody, *Working Women: The Subterranean World of Street Prostitution* (1985); Frederique Delacoste and Prescilla Alexander, *Sex Work: Writings By Women in the Sex Industry* (1987); Cecilie Hoigard and Liv Finstad, *Backstreets: Prostitution, Money and Love* (1986); Barbara M. Hobson, *Uneasy Virtue: The Politics of Prostitution and the American Reform Tradition* (1987); Glen Petri, *A Singular Iniquity: The Campaigns of Josephine Butler* (1971); Gail Pheterson, *A Vindication of the Rights of Whores* (1989); Maimie Pinzer, *The Maimie Papers* (Ruth Rosen ed., 1977); Kathleen Barry, "Social Etiology of Crimes Against Women," 10 *Victimology: An Int'l J.* 164 (1985); M.H. Silbert and A.M. Pines, "Early Sexual Exploitation as an Influence in Prostitution," *Soc. Work*, July-Aug. 1983, at 285; Judith Walkowitz, "The Politics of Prostitution," in *Women, Sex and Sexuality* 145 (Catherine R. Stimpson and Ethel S. Person eds., 1980); M.H. Silbert and A.M. Pines, "Occupational Hazards of Street Prostitutes," 8 *Crim. Just. & Behavior* 395 (1981); Belinda Cooper, "Prostitution: A Feminist Analysis," 11 *Women's Rts. L. Rep.* 99 (Summer 1989); Evelina Giobbe, WHISPER (Women Hurt in Systems of Prostitution Engaged in Revolt)(Educational Programs and Materials, Minneapolis, MN), Winter/Spring 1992; Andrea Dworkin, Address at

the Michigan Univ. School of Law Conference on Prostitution (Oct. 31, 1992).

13. See Adler, supra note 3; A.M. Brodsky, *Women in Prison— The Lonely Minority* (1975); Simon and Landis, supra note 3; Smart, supra note 3; Snow, supra note 3; *FBI Uniform Crime Reports* (1970-1989). According to a recent *New York Times* article, the arrest rates of women are rising more rapidly than men's. "During the 1980s, the number of women in state and federal prisons more than tripled, to 40,566; but the number of imprisoned men more than doubled, to 669,498. There are now approximately 90,000 women in state and federal prisons, and in city and county jails." Peter Applebome, "U.S. Prisons Challenged by Women Behind Bars," *N.Y. Times*, Nov. 30, 1992, at A10.

14. See Phyllis Chesler, *Women and Madness,* supra note 5; Phyllis Chesler, *Women, Money and Power* (1976).

15. See Chesler, *Women and Madness*, supra, note 5; Chesler, *Women, Money and Power*, supra note 14.

16. Hedda Nussbaum, formerly a children's book editor in New York City, was a battered common-law wife who failed to protect the illegally adopted five-year-old Lisa Steinberg from being tortured and ultimately killed by her common-law husband, former criminal defense attorney Joel Steinberg. See Gary Spencer, "Steinberg Conviction Affirmed," *N.Y.L.J.*, June 12, 1992, at 1; see also *People v. Steinberg*, 79 N.Y.2d 673, 584 N.Y.S.2d 770 (1992).

17. Mary Beth Whitehead was the New Jersey woman who, in 1985, signed a surrogacy contract to bear a child for William and Betsy Stern, and then changed her mind. In 1988, the New Jersey Supreme Court overturned Baby M's adoption by Betsy Stern and allowed Whitehead to have visitation. See *Matter of Baby M.*, 537 A.2d 1227 (Sup. Ct. N.J. 1988).

18. Amy Fisher, a teenager from Long Island, New York,

became sexually involved with Joseph Buttafuoco, a married man twice her age, when she was 15 to 16 years old. He prostituted her and then allegedly asked her to kill his wife, Mary Jo. Amy shot Mary Jo Buttafuoco on May 19, 1992. To date, Joey Buttafuoco has not been charged with statutory rape or with introducing Amy Fisher to a life of prostitution. See Shirley E. Perlman and Stuart Vincent, "Buttafuoco Won't Be Prosecuted in Amy Fisher Case, Nassau DA Says," *Newsday*, Oct. 23, 1992, at 3. The 17-year-old Fisher was sentenced to 5 to 15 years. See John T. McQuiston, "Amy Fisher Gets a Maximum of 15 Years," *N.Y. Times*, Dec. 2, 1992, at B1. In addition, CBS/Tri-Star Pictures reportedly paid the Buttafuocos between $200,000 and $300,000 for the rights to their story. NBC/KLM reportedly paid the Fishers $80,000. See Jeff Silverman, "Murder, Mayhem Stalk TV," *N.Y. Times*, Nov. 22, 1992, at H1, H28.

19. Imelda Marcos was the wife of the late Ferdinand Marcos, former President of the Phillipines. Ferdinand was apparently defeated in the 1986 presidential vote, during which his government was accused of fraud and intimidation, and later unseated by a popular uprising. See "Aquino Rejects Latest Calls for Marcos Burial in the Phillipines," *N.Y. Times*, Sept. 29, 1989, at B6. Imelda and Ferdinand were later brought up on racketeering charges involving fraud and embezzlement in assembling a "New York real estate empire." See "The Message of the Marcos Case," *N.Y. Times*, Nov. 1, 1988, at A30.

20. Leona Helmsley, 71-year-old millionairess, "queen" of the Helmsley hotel chain, was convicted on tax fraud charges and sentenced to four years in prison. See Constance L. Hays, "Helmsley Conviction Upheld on Appeal," *N.Y. Times*, July 31, 1991, at B2, col. 5.

21. Michael Milken was indicted in March, 1989 on 98 counts of fraud and racketeering in connection with insider trading and other alleged securities violations. See "The Milken

Sentence; Milken: Pathfinder for the 'Junk Bond Era'," *N.Y. Times*, Nov. 22, 1990, at D4. Milken later agreed to a plea bargain and entered guilty pleas to six felonies in addition to paying $600 million in penalties. Id. He was sentenced to ten years in prison, three years probation, and 5,400 hours of community service. Id.

22. Ivan Boesky pleaded guilty to insider trading in 1986. See Kurt Eichenwald, Drexel Burnham Fights Back, *N.Y. Times*, Sept. 11, 1988, 3, at 1. "The arbitrage king...admitted using information about unannounced takeovers to make huge illegal profits." Karen W. Arenson, "How Wall Street Bred an Ivan Boesky," *N.Y. Times*, Nov. 23, 1986, 3, at 1.

23. Neil Bush, youngest son of former president Bush, agreed to pay $50,000 in a settlement with federal regulators for his role in the collapse of the Silverado Banking, Savings and Loan Association, of which he was a director from 1985 to 1988. See Jeff Gerth, "The 1992 Campaign; The Business Dealings of the President's Relatives: What the Record Shows," *N.Y. Times*, Apr. 19, 1992, 1, at 14.

24. Sol Wachtler, former Chief Judge of the New York State Court of Appeals, was charged in a federal indictment of February 1, 1993 with extortion, mailing threatening letters to his ex-lover and her daughter, and lying to federal investigators. See Wayne King, "Ex-Chief Judge Pleads Not Guilty to Extortion," *N.Y. Times*, Feb. 18, 1993, at B6. "[T]he indictment charges that Mr. Wachtler used 'his power, influence, and resources as chief judge' to advance the extortion plan." Id. He faces as much as sixteen years in prison and $1.25 million in fines. Id.

25. Bess Myerson, former Miss America and New York City Cultural Affairs Commissioner, was brought up on federal fraud and conspiracy charges, together with a certain Mr. Capasso and Hortense Gabel, a former justice of the State Supreme Court in Manhattan. See Robert D. McFadden,

"Bess Myerson Is Accused of Shoplifting," *N.Y. Times*, May 28, 1988, 1, at 29. The three were accused of trying to reduce alimony payments in Mr. Capasso's divorce case and were acquitted on all charges in December of 1988. See "Headliners: The Envelope Please," *N.Y. Times*, Dec. 25, 1988, 4, at 7. In addition, Myerson was arrested in a small town in Pennsylvania for shoplifting $44.07 worth of goods. See McFadden, supra.

26. See Freda Adler and Rita James Simon, *The Criminology of Deviant Women*, 273-86 (1979); Chesler, *Mothers on Trial*, supra note 9; Richard DeMihg, *Women: The New Criminals* 170 (1977); Jones, supra note 3, at 293; Sarah K. Feeney and Samuel Roll, "Sex As an Extra Legal Factor in Judicial Decision-Making: An Analogous Study," 2 *Am. J. Forensic Psychol.* (1984).

27. Gender Bias Rep., supra note 11, at 87.

28. Id. at 93-97; Susan K. Datesman and Frank R. Scarpitti eds., (1980) *Women, Crime and Justice*, 325.

29. See Tape of Conference on Self-Defense and Battered Women, The Frontiers of Legal Thought: Race, Gender and Justice, held by the Duke Univ. Law Conference (Jan. 1991) [hereinafter Conference, Race, Gender and Justice](on file with Duke University Law School).

30. Gender Bias Rep., supra note 11, at 99-100 (text renumbered). Additionally, inmates at the Kentucky Correctional Institute for Women indicated that jail facilities in some rural counties are not equipped to adequately house females due to limited space and/or lack of female guards. As a result, female services or privileges, such as laundry and showers, are not available to female inmates with the frequency that they are provided to male inmates. It appears then that, in some rural areas where adequate space and staff are not available to house female prisoners, men may receive harsher penalties at sentencing, but women experience greater deprivation if actually incarcerated.

The inmates' complaints as to the inadequacy of jail space for women were echoed by testimony at the public hearings.

Another problem related to the lack of resources and jail space for women offenders is that because some states have fewer correctional institutions for women, incarcerated women who are mothers are frequently housed a considerable geographical distance from their children.

Gender Fairness in the Courts, supra note 11, at 34-35.

31. See Gillespie, supra note 4; Conference, Race, Gender and Justice, supra note 29.

32. See Browne, supra note 4; Conference, Race, Gender and Justice, supra note 29.

33. See Chesler, *Mothers on Trial*, supra note 9, at 66. Nonviolent mothers lose custody when it is contested from 70% to 82% of the time, often because they are nonviolent and unwilling to employ violent means in order to win custody of their children. Id.; Conference, Race, Gender and Justice, supra note 29.

34. I am not talking about female sexual outlaws: women who are "sexual" outside of marriage, women who use birth control, have abortions, or are prostitutes and/or lesbians.

35. See, e.g., Browne, supra note 4.

36. See, e.g., Gillespie, supra note 4.

37. See, e.g., Jones, supra note 4.

38. See, e.g., Schechter, supra note 4.

39. See, e.g., Elizabeth M. Scheider and Susan B. Jordan, Representation of Women Who Defend Themselves in Response to Physical or Sexual Assault, 4 *Women's Rts. L. Rep.* 149 (1978).

40. See, e.g., Diana E.H. Russell and Nicole Van den Ven, *The Proceedings of the International Tribunal on Crimes Against Women* (1976) (discussing congresses on crimes

against women and women's rights).

41. See, e.g., Walker, *The Battered Woman*, supra note 4; Walker, *Terrifying Love*, supra note 4.

42. See Jurik and Winn, supra note 4; Mann, "Black Women Who Kill," supra note 3; Scutt, supra note 4, at 271.

43. Monique Wittig, *Les Guerilleres* (1969).

44. Monique Wittig, *Across the Acheron* (1987).

45. Nawal el Sadawi, *Woman at Point Zero* (1975).

46. Joanna Russ, *The Female Man* (1976).

47. Marge Piercy, *Woman on the Edge of Time* (1976).

48. Suzy McKee Charnes, *Mother-Lines* (1976).

49. Sally Gearheart, *The Wanderground* (1976).

50. Kate Millet, *The Basement—Meditations on a Human Sacrifice* (1979).

51. Margaret Atwood, *The Handmaid's Tale* (1985).

52. Jeannette Winterson, *Sexing the Cherry* (1989).

53. Helen Zahavi, *The Weekend* (1991).

54. Diana Rivers, *Daughters of the Great Star* (1992).

55. Andrea Dworkin, *Mercy* (1990).

56. Id. at 331.

57. See Hickey, supra note 8, at 86.

58. See Ann W. Burgess et al, *Serial Rapists and Their Victims*, supra note 7; Cameron and Frazer, supra note 8; Caputi, supra note 8, at 202; Hickey, supra note 8, at 223; Malette et al., supra note 8; Jay Mathews, "San Diego Task Force Joins Search for Seattle-Area Killer," *Wash. Post*, Sept. 20, 1988, at A6; Baldwin, supra note 9, at 70.

59. See Hickey, supra note 8, at 223; Baldwin, supra note 10,

at 138.

60. See Aileen Carol Wuornos, Confession (Jan. 16, 1991)(transcript/videotape on file with author).

61. See "Highlights of the Wuornos Trial" (Court TV television broadcast, Jan. 1991) (Channel 51).

62. Wuornos, supra note 60.

63. Aileen Carol Wuornos, Testimony (Jan. 25, 1992).

64. Wuornos, supra note 60.

65. Id.

66. Gilfolye cites to a number of early to mid-nineteenth-century cases: *People v. Mott*, Oct. 20, 1842; *People v. Ford*, Sept. 28, 1842; *People v. Valentine*, Mar. 11, 1842; *People v. Golding*, Feb. 11, 1842; *People v. Wilson*, Jan. 9, 1840; *People v. Samis*, Feb. 20, 1837; *People v. Chichester*, May 11, 1836; *People v. Cole*, Dec. 16, 1836; *People v. Dikeman*, Dec. 14, 1836; *People v. Harrison*, May 12, 1833; *People v. Nosworthy*, Mar. 12, 1832; *Weyman v. Danon*, Dec. 12, 1832; *People v. Lozier*, June 14, 1831; *People v. Van Dine*, Jan. 7, 1831; *People v. Small*, Jan. 16, 1829; *People v. Anderson*, Jan. 12, 1829; *People v. Fink*, July 14, 1825; *People v. Lee*, Dec. 15, 1824; *People v. Johnson*, Jan. 9, 1821; *People v. Halliday*, Mar. 11, 1820.

67. See Gilfoyle, supra note 6, at 78-79.

John Evans, for example, was arrested for throwing stones at the house of Eliza Vincent after she "refused him admittance." Similarly, James Van Dine broke into Rebecca Weyman's house "by forcing open the windows and shutters...there behaved in a most riotous and disorderly manner." Similarly, Hannah Fuller was awakened by William Ford early one summer morning in 1844. After kicking in her door, he removed his boots and pants, carried her to the bed, and attempted "to ravish and...carnally know her." Only the last-minute intervention by the watch prevented the rape. Fuller later dropped the charges because Ford was an "old friend."

Women on the street had even less protection from such assaults. Mary Smith, a Leonard Street prostitute, was walking home in 1832 after an evening at the Park Theater when William Nosworthy seized her "in a grossly rude and indecent manner and raised her clothes so as to expose her nakedness to the passers by."

Id. at 79.

68. See Gilfoyle, supra note 6, at 79-80.

The three rioters who stoned Amanda Smith's house on Franklin Street also "destroyed her furniture, knocked her down, beat her on the face and head so as to blind her entirely, and after having knocked her down, kicked her." The invaders, charged the district attorney, then beat her crippled son William "in a most shameful and outrageous manner." Witnesses testified that the same men forced their way into two other Orange Street brothels, "making a great noise and disturbance, breaking the furniture." Likewise, John Golding led four other men into Elizabeth Rinnell's Crosby Street house and demanded food, drink, money, and entertainment. After their drunken orgy, Golding assaulted and beat Rinnell. Similarly, when John Williams entered an Anthony Street brothel, he threw oil of vitriol in Mary Ann Duffy's face, severely scarring her. And when Edward Halliday and friends broke into a Bancker Street house, each one "drew a sword and slashed before them, [and] wounded Sarah Smith, the woman of the house, in the face."

The threat of rape was common in many of these brothel riots. Five men, for example, broke into Eliza Logue's Thomas Street house when she refused them admittance. After breaking the cookery and throwing a lamp at the head of a prostitute, they strangled Logue and "threw her across the foot of a bed and endeavored by force and violence to have connection with her." Only the nearby watch,

145

hearing the commotion, prevented the consummation of the act. In 1840, after beating Mary Lee, Benjamin Waldron and his gang followed her as she tried to escape, striking "her in the face several times and threaten[ing] to commit other outrages." In another instance, more than ten laborers broke into Eliza Ann Potter's Suffolk Street house, violently assaulted her, and "threatened to pickle and rape her before hastily departing."

Id. at 80-81.

69. Id. at 84-85.

70. Id. at 90.

71. Susan Hunter et al. *Council For Prostitution Alternatives, Inc. Annual Report* (1991).

72. Id. at 2.

73. Id.

74. Id. at 3.

75. Gender Bias Rep., supra note 10, at 179-80.

76. Phillipa Levine, *Prostitution in Florida—A Report Presented to the Gender Bias Study Commission of the Supreme Court of Florida* 34-35 (Sept. 1988).

77. Id. at 43.

78. See Dorothy H. Bracey, "Concurrent and Consecutive Abuse: The Juvenile Prostitute," in *The Criminal Justice System and Women* 317, 321 (Barbara Raffel Price and Natalie J. Sokoloff eds., 1982) (indicating risk of physical abuse and mugging); Dorothy H. Bracey, *Baby-Pros: Preliminary Profiles of Juvenile Prostitutes* 62-63 (1979).

79. Eleanor M. Miller, *Street Woman* 138 (1986).

80. See Bracey, supra note 78, at 317 ("[a] growing body of evidence [indicates] that the juvenile [prostitute]...is the product of a specific history...that most likely involves sex-

ual abuse, incest, ...[and] abandonment"); Bracey, supra note 78, at 62-63; Jennifer James, "Motivations for Entrance into Prostitution," in *The Female Offender*, 177 (L. Crites ed., 1976) ("Prostitutes are not the cause of prostitution."); Jennifer James and Jane Meyerding, "Early Sexual Experience as a Factor in Prostitution," 7 *Archives of Sexual Behavior* 31-42 (1978); Richard Phillips, "How Children Become Prostitutes," *Chi. Trib.*, Feb. 1, 1981, 12, (quoting Mimi Silbert); Bernie Schaffer and Richard R. DeBlassie, "Adolescent Prostitution," 19 *Adolescence* 689, 689-696 (1984); Carmen and Moody, supra note 12 (chronicling church and social work with prostitutes); Mimi H. Silbert and Ayala M. Pines, "Entrance Into Prostitution," 13 *Youth & Soc'y* 471, 479 (1982) (tabulating statistics on physical and sexual child abuse).

81. Letter from Susan Kay Hunter, Executive Director, Council for Prostitution Alternatives, to Phyllis Chesler (Jan. 6, 1993) (on file with author).

82. See Silbert and Pines, *Occupational Hazards of Street Prostitutes*, supra note 12, at 397.

83. Id.

84. Baldwin, supra note 10.

85. For more information on the trauma of sexual and pyschological abuse, see E. Sue Blume, *Secret Survivors: Uncovering Incest and its Aftereffects in Women* (1990); Sandra Butler, *Conspiracy of Silence: The Trauma of Incest* (1985); Phyllis Chesler, *Sacred Bond—The Legacy of Baby M.* (1988) (psychological consequences of surrendering a child to adoption); Judith Louis Herman, *Trauma and Recovery* (1992); Marian Sandmaier, *The Invisible Alcoholics: Women and Alcohol Abuse in America* (1980); Bessel A. Van de Kolk, *Psychological Trauma* (1987); Gail Wyatt and Gloria Johnson Powell, *Lasting Effects of Child Sexual Abuse* (1988); Roland Summit, "The Child Sexual Abuse Accommodation Syndrome," 7 *Child Abuse and*

Neglect, 177–193 (1983); see also Ellen Bass and Laura Davis, *The Courage to Heal: A Guide for Women Survivors of Child Sexual Abuse* (1988); Toni Ann Laidlaw and Cheryl Malmo, *Healing Voices: Feminist Approach To Therapy With Women* (1990).

86. See Don R. Kates and Nancy Jean Engberg, "Deadly Force Self-Defense Against Rape," 15 *U.C. Davis L. Rev.* 873, 873-74 (1982) ("Resistance short of homicide is clearly condoned. Moreover, American law...has always recognized a right to use deadly force if reasonably necessary to prevent rape.") The experts I chose and proposed to the defense either wrote the following books and conducted the following studies, or were knowledgeable about the information contained therein: Louise Armstrong, *Kiss Daddy Goodnight* (1978); Pauline B. Bart and Patricia H. O'Brien, *Stopping Rape—Successful Survival Strategies* (1985); Katherine Brady, *Father's Days: A True Story of Incest* (1979); Gillespie, supra note 4; Margaret T. Gordon and Stephanie Riger, *The Female Fear—The Social Cost of Rape* (1989) (tabulating case studies on rape and fear of crime); Judith Louis Herman, *Father-Daughter Incest* (1981); Liz Kelly, *Surviving Sexual Violence* (1988) (chronicling wife abuse, child abuse, and family violence in the United States); Dean H. Knudsen and JoAnn L. Miller, *Abused and Battered: Social and Legal Responses to Family Violence* (1991); Lee Madigan and Nancy Gamble, *The Second Rape—Society's Continued Betrayal of the Victim* (1991); Florence Rush, *The Best Kept Secret: Sexual Abuse of Children* (1980); Russell and Van den Ven, supra note 40; Diana E.H. Russell, *Rape in Marriage* (1982); Peggy Reeves Sanday, *Fraternity Gang Rape: Sex, Brotherhood, and Privilege on Campus* (1990); Diana Scully, *Understanding Sexual Violence: A Study of Convicted Rapists* (1990); Walker, *Terrifying Love*, supra note 4; Judith Fabricant, "Homicide in Response to a Threat of Rape: A Theoretical Examination of the Rule of Justification," 11 *Golden Gate U.L. Rev.* 945, 947 (1981)

(identifying historical background of attempted rape as justification for homicide); Laura E. Reece, "Women's Defenses to Criminal Homicide and the Right to Effective Assistance of Counsel: The Need for Relocation of Difference," 1 *UCLA Women's L.J.* 1101 (1991); Laurie J. Taylor, "Provoked Reason in Men and Women: Heat-of-Passion Manslaughter and Imperfect Self-Defense," 33 *UCLA L. Rev.* 1679, 1679 (1986) ("legal standards that define...provocation...reflect a male view"); see also supra note 85.

87. Telephone Interview with Aileen Carol Wuornos (Apr. 1991).

88. See Chesler, *Women and Madness*, supra note 6, at 138 ("prostitution, rape, and sexual molestation of female children by adult males are so common they are usually invisible"); Herman, supra note 85, at 87; Van de Kolk, supra note 85.

89. Such inquiry would not have implicated the "rape shield" laws, which prevent the use of evidence of the victim's past sexual conduct in rape cases. See Ann Althouse, "Thelma and Louise and the Law: Do Rape Shield Rules Matter?" 25 *Loy. L.A. L. Rev.* 757 (1992); Letter from Margaret Baldwin to Susan Bender, President of the Women's Bar Association of the State of New York (Nov. 1992)(on file with author). Professor Baldwin stated:

> During the course of the William Kennedy Smith Trial, it became very clear to me that the rape shield rule had been taken as a hostage to guarantee silence about men, as in "if you don't have to tell, neither do we." This is phony symmetry, but one that has garnered strong surface appeal. Formal logic, like formal equality, has never interested me terribly. What has interested me profoundly in this turn of events is the whole question of "shield rules" that run to the benefit of men as johns: never arrested, never held to

account, while the prostitutes who might give witness are discredited when not wholly destroyed. It bears mention that johns are commonly white, middle-aged, married men with some disposable income; that is, real people.

90. See Horzepa deposition, infra note 96.

91. See Deposition, infra note 96.

92. See Robert Nolin, "Jurors Seated for Wuornos Trial," *Daytona Beach News J.*, Jan. 15, 1992, at B1.

93. See Laura Kauffman, "Dancer's Story Adds Twist to Killing," *Ocala Star-Banner*, Jan. 5, 1992, at 1A.

94. Id.

95. Nancy Peterson appeared on NBC-Dateline on November 10, 1992. See NBC Dateline (NBC television broadcast, Nov. 10, 1992).

96. See Deposition of Lawrence Peter Horzepa (Oct. 15, 1991), *State v. Wuornos* (7th Jud. Cir., Volusia Co., Fla. 1992) (No. 91-0257).

Horzepa told Jenkins:
In speaking to Jackie Davis, which was the last known girlfriend of Mr. Mallory, she also said that he would like to drink, he enjoyed the strip bars, he was into some pornography....
...We found that in doing a search of the business that he appeared to be heavy in debt; he owed several thousand dollars for the rental of the store-front property that he had. We found hostile notes from customers who had dropped items to be repaired, which he apparently never did, and they were calling back or writing notes—apparently he wasn't returning phone calls—asking when they were going to get their items back. We took a look and saw over a hundred items that

were in need of repair which he hadn't even started to work on. We found correspondence from IRS. Apparently he was in trouble with them, and he was, appeared to be, looked like he was going to be audited.

Jenkins asked:

I know ultimately you had a suspect...Chastity Marcus.... And how exactly did you get to her?

Horzepa replied:

It was from—we had found some notes, handwritten notes, on a scrap piece of paper that were found in [Mallory's] living quarters....

[Marcus] had told us that she had had a date with Mr. Mallory, her and Kimberly Guy. And I asked her what "a date" meant, and she told me that "a date" to her and Kimberly Guy was that they went back to his place of business and had sex with him....And I asked her if she received payment for this service, and she said that she did, that it was in the form of a 19-inch color TV and a VCR...probably somebody's that were there for repair.... Chastity Marcus was fuzzy on [the date]. Kimberly Guy, to the best of her knowledge, thought that it was the evening of November 30th.

...[Kimberly Guy] advised that she was a lesbian and that she had a lesbian lover. She brought us over to her apartment where there had been a TV and VCR she had claimed that Mr. Mallory had given her.

97. I had three meetings with Jenkins and a conversation with investigator Don Sanchez in the spring of 1991 about this. I again referred to the need to delve into Mallory's past violence toward women in a letter to Jenkins dated June 12, 1991. See Letter from Phyllis Chesler to Trish Jenkins, Public Defender, Marion County (June 12, 1991)(on file with author); Interviews with Patricia Jenkins, Public

Defender, Marion County (Apr. to May 1991); Interviews with Donald Sanchez, Private Investigator for Marion County Office of the Public Defender (Apr. to May 1991).

98. I obtained Richard Mallory's criminal record from the Circuit Court, Montgomery County, Maryland. In 1957, Mallory entered the home of a woman married to a wealthy and powerful man and attempted to rape her. He did not succeed. It is puzzling that in 1957, a young white man was actually convicted for attempted rape, sentenced to four, and ultimately imprisoned for 10 years. Class and race biases always predominate in determining which man actually gets arrested and convicted for a crime of sexual violence against a woman.

99. Telephone Interview with Jack Kassewitz, Private Investigator for NBC Broadcasting, (Nov. 5, 1992). Kassewitz boasted that it took him "about 20 minutes" to commandeer Mallory's record. Id.

100. NBC-Dateline (NBC television broadcast, Nov. 10, 1992).

101. Id.

102. *Question of Silence* (directed by Marleen Gorris, 1983).

103. The most idealistic and hard-working of public defenders is still too overworked and lacks the resources to do more than a perfunctory job. At the time of her assignment, Trish Jenkins was defending 12 other capital cases. Her pre-trial motions for continuances in the Wuornos case invariably met with unnecessarily acerbic opposition from the state, so much so that at one hearing, exasperated, she asked the judge: "Do I spend all my time on Ms. Wuornos' case and let the others slide? Or do I do it in reverse? I am in a bind."

104. See Michael Clary, "A Mother's Love," *L.A. Times*, Dec. 17, 1991, at E1, (quoting Phyllis Chesler on subject); Laura Kauffmann, "Wuornos: Victim of Society?" *Ocala Star Banner*, Dec. 11, 1991, at 1A (same); Chris Lavin, "Deaths Fade in Backdrop as Trial Takes Center Stage," *St.*

Petersberg Times, Jan. 12, 1991 (same); Keith Maranger, "Trial Begins for Lesbian Serial Killer," *Our Town*, Feb. 1992, at 1 (same).

105. For an expansion on these points, see Phyllis Chesler, "A Double Standard for Murder?" *N.Y. Times*, Jan. 8, 1992, at A19.

106. See Wuornos, supra note 60.

107. See "Highway Slayings May Go Hollywood," *Sun-Sentinel*, Feb. 10, 1991, at 20A. Maj. Dan Henry later resigned after the release of a taped telephone conversation in which he discussed depositions taken for a civil lawsuit between Wuornos and a Hollywood filmmaker and producer. See "Deputy Resigns After Conversation About Wuornos," *Miami Herald*, Nov. 12, 1992, at 2B. In an early version of the CBS script, *Overkill: The Aileen Wuornos Story*, the only names not fictionalized were Moore's, Munster's, Binegar's, and Henry's.

108. See "Movie Deal 'Didn't Prejudice' Probe," *Miami Herald*, Dec. 4, 1991, at 1B.

109. Telephone Interviews with Steven Glazer, Defense Attorney for Aileen Carol Wuornos (Mar. 1992 to Nov. 1992).

110. Id. Numerous newspaper and magazine articles and two books on the Wuornos case have already appeared: Dolores Kennedy and Robert Nolin, *On A Killing Day* (1992) and Michael Reynolds, *Dead Ends* (1992). A number of television programs about Wuornos have aired, some repeatedly. Court TV aired highlights of the January 1992 trial proceedings; in depth features appeared on "A Current Affair," "Inside Edition," Montel Williams, NBC-Dateline (August and November, 1992). The Republic Pictures/CBS Movie *Overkill: The Aileen Wuornos Story* appeared on CBS on Nov. 17, 1992.

Wuornos actually attracted a minimal amount of money. The three sheriffs and Tyria Moore allegedly shared

$200,000 from CBS/Republic Pictures; Wuornos, to the best of my knowledge, has received and dispersed to others between $30,000 and $40,000.

111. Judge Graziano recused herself in December 1991, about three weeks before trial.

112. Telephone Interview with Dawn Botkins, Michigan resident and childhood friend of Wuornos (Nov. to Dec. 1992); Communications with Arlene Pralle, Florida resident and adoptive parent of Wuornos (Apr. 1991 to Mar. 1992); Communications with Aileen Carol Wuornos (Apr. 1991 to Dec. 1992).

113. See "'Fascinated' By a Famous Killer," *Atlanta J. & Const.*, Jan. 29, 1992, at A2.

114. See Larry Keller, "Victims," *Sun-Sentinel*, Jan. 24, 1989, at 1A.

115. See Rule, supra note 8, at 360. Many lawyers are horrified by how grievously the state of Florida has gone about violating Wuornos's civil and constitutional rights. Early on, in the spring of 1991, lawyer Linda Backiel led me to Len Weinglas who agreed to defend Wuornos pro bono in the first of her six trials, but who needed at least $50,000 in expense money. Once I became ill with Chronic Fatigue Immune Dysfunction Syndrome, I could no longer continue fundraising. No one else ever took on this enormous, exhausting, and volunteer responsibility.

However, a number of lawyers have since expressed interest in the case and are willing to write amicus briefs and assist counsel pro bono: Margaret Baldwin, Professor of Law, Tallahassee Law School; The New York State Women's Bar Association, especially Naomi Werne, Chair of the Criminal Law Committee; Alan Dershowitz of the Harvard Law School; Ruthann Robson, Professor of Law at CUNY Law School. Nevertheless, despite at least 50 or 60 requests for pro bono assistance, no one lawyer ever agreed to take responsibility for coordinating a legal team or for the remaining trial work.

116. See *Williams v. State*, 110 So. 2d 654, 662 (Fla. 1959). The Williams rule provides for the admission of evidence of a defendant's other crimes or alleged crimes if the court determines that the facts are sufficiently similar to show a common scheme or pattern. Id.

117. James G. Driscoll, "In Smith Trial, Legal System Forced Jurors to Operate Partially in the Dark," *Sun-Sentinel*, Dec. 15, 1991, at 7G.

118. According to Florida law, the jury first determines guilt or innocence and, if guilty, then makes an initial sentencing recommendation to the judge, who may override that recommendation. See *Parker v. Dugger*, 111 S.Ct. 731, 735 (1991); Fla. Stat. ch. 921 (1991).

119. Telephone Interview with Dr. Lenore Walker, author of *Terrifying Love: Why Battered Women Kill and How Society Responds* and *The Battered Woman* (Dec. 1991).

120. See "Prosecutor Who Prayed With Bundy To Leave Ministry," *Sun-Sentinel*, Jan. 29, 1989, at 17A.

121. See Phil Long, "Prostitute Called Abused Victim, Enraged Killer," *Miami Herald*, Jan. 16, 1992, at 1A.

122. Deposition of Elizabeth McMahon (Jan. 8, 1991), *State v. Wuornos*, (7th Jud. Cir., Volusia Co., Fla. 1992)(No. 91-0257).

123. Robert Nolin, "Wuornos Described as 'Borderline'," *Daytona News Journal*, Jan. 29, 1992, at 1B.

124. See Phyllis Chesler, "Sex, Death and the Double Standard," *On The Issues* (Summer 1992) (comparing Wuornos's treatment with that of Bundy).

125. See Laura Kauffmann, "Wuornos' Brother Disputes Abuse Tale," *Ocala-Star Banner*, Jan. 30, 1992, at 1A.

126. Telephone Interview with Steven Glazer, Defense Attorney

for Aileen Carol Wuornos (Mar. 1, 1992). While Glazer's behavior may be legal, I must question whether it is ethical—especially since Glazer agreed to represent Wuornos civilly as well as criminally.

127. See supra note 6 and accompanying text.

128. See, e.g., *People v. Matthews*, 154 Cal. Rptr. 628, 629-30 (Ct. App. 1979); *People v. Taylor*, 9 Cal. Rptr. 390, 391-93 (Ct. App. 1960); *State v. Harris*, 222 N.W.2d 462 (Iowa 1974); *Commonwealth v. Lamrini*, 467 N.E.2d 95, 97-98 (Mass. 1984); *People v. Heflin*, 456 N.E.2d 10, 12-13 (Mich. 1990), rev'g *People v. Landrum*, 407 N.W.2d 614, 615-16 (Mich. Ct. App. 1986); *People v. Barker*, 446 N.W.2d 549, 550 (Mich. Ct. App. 1989), aff'd 468 N.W.2d 492, 493 (Mich. 1991); *State v. Goodseal*, 183 N.W.2d 258, 260-61 (Neb. 1971), cert. denied, 404 U.S. 845 (1971); *People v. Williams*, 553 N.Y.S.2d 818, 819 (N.Y. App. Div. 1990); *Commonwealth v. Carbone*, 544 A.2d 462, 463-64 (Pa. Super. Ct. 1988), rev'd, 574 A.2d 584, 588 (Pa. 1990); *Thomas v. State*, 578 S.W. 2d 691, 694-95 (Tex. Crim. App. 1979).

129. See *State v. Wanrow*, 538 P.2d 849 (Wash. Ct. App. 1975), aff'd, 559 P.2d 548 (Wash. 1977) (en banc).

130. See Morris Dees, *A Season for Justice: A Lawyer's Own Story of Victory Over America's Hate Groups* (1991). Joan Little was a black woman who killed a white jail guard who attempted to rape her in the jail cell in which she was incarcerated for a burglary conviction. She was acquitted in 1975 following a capital murder trial that attracted national attention. *State v. Little*, 74 Cr. No. 4176 (Superior Court, Beaufort County, N.C. 1975).

131. See *People v. Garcia*, 126 Cal. Rptr. 275 (Ct. App. 1976), cert. denied, 426 U.S. 911 (1976); see also Kenneth W. Salter, *The Trial of Inez Garcia* (1976).

132. 559 P.2d 548 (Wash. 1977).

133. Id. at 559.

134. Id. at 550.

135. Additionally, Ms. Hooper had noticed someone prowling around her house at night a week earlier, and someone had slashed her bedroom window screens in an attempt to enter the house only two days before; Ms. Hooper suspected that Wesler was responsible. Id. at 55.

136. Id. at 551.

137. Id. at 555.

138. Id. at 550.

139. Id. at 558-59.

140. Id. at 555.

141. Id. at 557.

142. Id. at 558.

143. Id.

144. Id. at 558-59. According to papers on file at the Center for Constitutional Rights in New York, Wanrow's second trial never happened. Wanrow pled guilty to reduced charges of manslaughter and second degree assault. She received two concurrent sentences of 10 and 20 years, which were simultaneously suspended, the period of suspension and termination being five years conditioned upon probation during this time—which probation apparently also eliminated a concurrent 12-month sentence. The Center for Constitutional Rights, 853 Broadway, New York, New York 10003.

145. At the risk of frustrating the reader, I have chosen to summarize and evaluate most of these articles at a later date. See generally Fabricant, supra note 86; Kates and Engberg, supra note 86; Mackinnon, infra note 148; Taylor, supra note 86; Reece, supra note 86; Schneider and Jordan, supra note 40; Lita Furby, et al. "Judged Effectiveness of

Common Rape Prevention and Self-Defense Strategies," 4 *J. Interpersonal Violence* 44 (1989); Julie Blackman, "Potential Uses for Expert Testimony: Ideas Toward the Representation of Battered Women Who Kill," 9 *Women's Rts. L. Rep.* 227 (1986); Morrison Torrey, "When Will We Be Believed? Rape Myths and the Idea of a Fair Trial in Rape Prosecutions," 24 *U.C. Davis L. Rev.*, 1013, 1013-71.

146. See Schneider and Jordan, supra note 39, at 156.

147. Id.

148. See Catherine MacKinnon, "Towards Feminist Jurisprudence," 34 *Stan. L. Rev.* 703, 729-30 (1982) (book review).

149. Id. at 734.

150. Schneider, "Representation of Women Who Defend Themselves in Response to Physical or Sexual Assault," *Women's Rights Law Reporter*, Vol. 4, No. 3, (Spring, 1978); Fabricant, "Homicide in Response to a Threat of Rape: A Theoretical Examination of the Rule of Justification," Vol. II, *Golden Gate University Law Review*, P. 945, (1981); Kates and Engberg, "Deadly Force Self-Defense Against Rape," (15) Univ. of CA Davis, 873, (1982); Mackinnon, "Toward Feminist Jurisprudence," *Stanford Law Review*, Volume 34, No. 3, (February 1982); Laurie J. Taylor, "Provoked Reason in Men and Women: Heat-of-Passion Manslaughter and Imperfect Self-Defense", 33 *UCLA L. REV.* 1679, (1986); Furby, Lita, et al., "Judged Effectiveness of Common Rape Prevention and Self-Defense Strategies," Eugene Research Institute., *Journal of Interpersonal Violence*, Vol. 4 No. 1, (March 1989); Laura E. Reece, Ibid. "Women's Defenses to Criminal Homicide and the Right to Effective Assistance of Counsel: The Need for Relocation of Difference," *UCLA Women's Law Journal*, Vol. 1, No. 1, (Spring, 1991); Torrey Morrison, "When Will We Be Believed? Rape

Myths and the Idea of a Fair Trial in Rape Prosecutions," *University of California, Davis Law Review*, Vol. 24:931, (1991); Naomi R. Cahn, "The Looseness of Legal Language: The Reasonable Woman Standard in Theory and in Practice," *Cornell Law Review*, Vol. 77:1398, (1992).

151. See *Coker v. Georgia*, 433 U.S. 584, 592 (1977).

152. See *People v. Caudillo*, 580 P.2d 274, 289 (Cal. 1978).

153. The government-subsidized "takeover" of the grass-roots shelter movement for battered women, with the co-operation of mental health professionals, made an open exchange of ideas even more difficult.

154. Based on an interview with G. Kristan Miccio, Director and Attorney-in-Charge, Sanctuary for Families and Center for Battered Women Legal Services, New York, NY.

155. See Schneider and Jordan, supra note 39; Walker, *The Battered Woman*, supra note 4; Walker, *Terrifying Love*, supra note 4; see Elizabeth Schneider, "Equal Rights To Trial for Women: Sex Bias in the Law of Self-Defense," 15 *Harv. C.R.-C.L. Rev.* 622, 630-47 (1980).

156. Communications with Arlene Pralle and Aileen Wuornos (1991).

157. Telephone Interview with Steven Glazer, Defense Attorney for Aileen Wuornos (Mar. 1, 1992).

158. See *Simon & Schuster, Inc. v. Members of the New York State Crime Victims Bd.*, 112 S.Ct. 501, 503 (1991)(holding New York's Son of Sam Law, which prevented people "accused or convicted of a crime" from profiting from their stories, as inconsistent with the First Amendment).

159. From April to July of 1991, Pralle often, and her husband once, asked me to provide Pralle with money to pay for Wuornos's collect phone calls. Pralle also asked me for valium for "bodily pains," for money to pay someone to help

her with her horse-farm work, and to consider moving in with her myself.

160. Wuornos stopped writing to me again as of December, 1992. Although she has complained bitterly about Steven Glazer, she has not fired him as her lawyer.

161. Laura Kauffmann, "Wuornos Asks Judge To End It All," *Ocala Star-Banner*, Apr. 1, 1992, at 1A, 6A.

162. Laura Kauffmann, "Wuornos To Return For Appeals," *Ocala Star-Banner*, Nov. 22, 1992, at 1A, 4A.

163. Communications with Aileen Wuornos, Steven Glazer, and Jaqui Giroux (1992).

164. See generally Herman, supra note 85.

Sister, Fear Has No Place Here

Some say lesbians are dangerous. I'd always hoped this was so, but time and experience soon taught me that lesbian—and for that matter, heterosexual feminists, are not always dangerous enough. Feminists of all sexual persuasions often sport a brand of politics more royalist than democratic, more academic than activist. And, like brotherhood, sisterhood is an ideal, not a reality; feminists are no more sisterly than anyone else is. Feminist homophobia, racism and misogyny have, over the years, driven many feminists out of coalitions and into "queer" or "racial" organizations—or back into civilian life.

It's hard to remain radical in feminist terms when, in addition to gender or skin-color, your sexual preference is also feared and hated, not only by your opponents, but by your comrades; it's hard to remain "in service" to others, when you yourself remain unsafe at every moment—which is precisely why Camp Sister Spirit in Ovett, Mississippi, (population 200), is so important. Brenda and Wanda Henson have not dropped out—nor have they sold out. They—and their full-time supporters: Pam Firth, Arthur Henson, Andrea Gibbs, Cheri Michael and Kathy Wilson, are maintaining a level of visibility and virtue that is almost pure science fiction.

Ovett is about 3 hours northeast of New Orleans, and

about 40 minutes northeast of Hattiesburg. Driving from New Orleans to Hattiesburg, I search the horizon for some sign that we're in the south: a bayou, a creek, a weeping willow. You can drive for miles and never know where you are, at any given moment you could be anywhere: in New England or in the Pacific Northwest, the same familiar chain-stores and motels you've just passed fifty or a hundred miles ago, are always waiting to greet you. For three thousand miles, it's as if you haven't left home; wherever you are, there's always a Holiday Inn, a Day's Inn, a Howard Johnson's, a Ramada Inn, a Burger King, a Wendy's, a McDonald's—it's as if there's nothing indigenous left in America, except the trees maybe, and the sky. Whoever's left is moving fast, hurtling forward into the future, on the great American highway.

At a local restaurant in Hattiesburg, a woman tells me she lives in Ovett. "Ovett?" I say. "Isn't that where Camp Sister Spirit is? What's going on there? "Oh", she sighs, "I think the media's been exaggerating things. Local folk—as long as you leave them alone, they'll leave you alone. Well," she says, lowering her voice, "truth is, they're very strict in Ovett. They're not as liberal as they make out. Things are real black and white. They're Baptist." (So much for media exaggeration). "I'm glad to meet someone from a big city. I miss that. I once spent some time in Chicago."

"Greyhound still goes to Chicago," I say.

"Oh, I can't leave" she says, in a resigned and matter-of-fact voice. "If you're married to a redneck, you can't go nowhere. And even if you do, he'll come after you and bring you back."

At another meal, in another restaurant, another hostage in Ovett says this: "Those women (at Camp Sister Spirit) are going to die. It's only a matter of time. Y'see, Ovett folk don't like outsiders and they don't like anyone who's different. The people in Ovett are crazy. They're all kin, or married to kin. Once, the phone company installed a phone booth in the center of town. Some of the boys just wrenched that booth loose, and towed it out of town, on top of their car."

Given the local attitudes, I found it remarkable that American feminists: lesbians mainly, but not exclusively, are risking their lives, not as saleable commodities, not for their own bedroom entertainment, not even for the sake of money, or careers, but for the right to practice feminism.

I wanted to meet the Hensons and their supporters, gauge who'd be there after the media and the federal mediators were gone, the initial money depleted, and the national community's attention diverted honorably elsewhere.

Volunteers Lucy, 37, a hairdresser, and a long-time abortion clinic defender from Sacramento, and Sasha, 23, a recent college graduate from Pittsburgh, drive us on the back roads from Hattiesburg to the camp. Our headlights are the only lights for miles around; there are no streetlights and few houses. Lucy makes casual conversation. "Yes, we still hear gunshots around the periphery of the property." Sasha says: "The fear we feel is so real, but we're learning to deal with it. The fear—you work it out by keeping busy. This creates a positive energy. It helps you distance yourself from what can happen."

Lucy cuts in to remind us: "Pam Firth, she's from Mississippi, she's here permanently, was shot at 5 times in a drive-by shooting. She had to jump into a ditch to avoid being killed. She tried to make a citizens arrest. It took a long while but now the police are at least charging the man, Marty Blackwell, with disturbing the peace."

There we are, myself, and my friends: unarmed visitors with over-active imaginations, being driven a long distance in the darkness, without guns, or walkie-talkies, trying to act safe, not scared. For one moment, I allow myself to feel terrified. It's not hard. Many warriors have both waged and ultimately lost the "good fight" in Mississippi. In the 1960's, civil rights workers were killed, their supporters' homes fire-bombed and their businesses ruined.

I think of Emmett Till, James Meredith, Medger Evers and Martin Luther King, of Violet Liuzzo, and especially of James Chaney, Micky Schwerner, and Andrew Goodman. I think of how in 1970, the Jackson city police attacked a black dormitory at Jackson State, killing two and wounding 12 students in their search for a sniper. Early in 1971, 20 acres had been purchased near Jackson for a separate nation, to be known as the Republic of New Africa. The FBI and the state police smashed the residences on the land, and arrested 11 people and sentenced all 11 to long prison terms for sedition.

I am carrying a book: it's Sojourner Truth's Narrative of her Life, recently published by the Schomburg Library of 19th century Black Women Writers. I touch it for courage. And I remind myself of the steadfast bravery of Mississippi black women like Fanny Lou Hamer, Ruby Doris Smith (Robinson), and Unita Blackwell, who is now the mayor of Taylorsville, and the extraordinary courage of all their local supporters.

In 1954, the recently deceased white journalist, Hazel Brannon Smith, condemned a local sheriff for shooting a young black man in the back. In 1964, Smith also became the first woman to win a Pulitzer Prize for her editorial crusading. But her newspaper, *The Advertiser*, was boycotted for ten years by local businesses and ultimately forced to close.

In the mid-to late 1980's, Mississippi mothers Karen Newsom and Dorrie Singley were forced to 'kidnap' their daughters and/or flee the state to rescue their (allegedly) sexually abused children from court-awarded paternal custody. Newsom was jailed in Forrest County. (The Hensons picketed the jail on her behalf.) Dorrie Singley died, while Underground; her lawyer, Garnett Harrison was disbarred for her role in the case and no longer practices law or lives in Mississippi. I half expect the Mississippi state police or the Klan or Church terrorists to suddenly stop our car, but no one does, and we proceed on to Camp Sister Spirit.

The moon's out, and it's enchanted. Twenty women, from at least 10 states, are sitting in an open-air circle in the sultry southern night. They introduce themselves by name, age (21 to 65), and sun sign, and when I mention that hours before I was hit on the head and neck in a freak accident, a woman immediately materializes out of the darkness and starts giving me a massage; someone else brings me ibuprofen and an ice pack. It's unimaginable that guns and hate are trained on women like these.

Camp Sister Spirit is like Woodstock, Lesbian Nation, and the Michigan Women's Music Festival, but it's also like Mississippi Freedom Summer, the Mothers of the Plaza de Mayo, a Goddess Grove, and a Girl Scout Camp. Ah, it's like nothing else. It's as if Diana Rivers' tale about a tribe of psychic-military lesbian feminist warriors (Daughters of the Great Star) has come to life, and I'm sitting with them. (Magically, Rivers herself is here too).

Camp Sister Spirit is not a young, Butch para-military encampment. True, there are swaggers, buzz cuts, muscles and bared breasts galore, but there are women in skirts and jewelry here too, women in their 50's and 60's, mothers and grandmothers with gray hair, and smiling wrinkles. No one has come here to die. They are here to support the kind of grass roots work that feminists have been doing for years.

We're so naive, so American, we don't believe we can be killed for our (feminist) beliefs, not in the land of the free, the home of the brave.

And yet, Camp Sister Spirit has been under siege since November, 1993. The Hensons and their supporters have become high-profile symbols of feminist resistance. I've waited 27 years to see feminists gathered together—not on television panels, or at conferences or parties, but on collectively owned land, taking a stand for what they believe in.

Brenda and Wanda Henson did not have confrontation in mind when they first bought these secluded, 120 acres. In fact, they wanted to get away from the harassment they'd previously suffered on rented campgrounds. Although the Henson's have painted the tractor and many trees (!) lavender, their version of feminism is essentially one of service. They're not "do me" feminists; they "do" food banks and clothes closets, they counsel battered women and incest and rape victims. After witnessing numerous prisoner-beatings and some so-called prisoner "suicides," including the "suicide" of the son of the President of the NAACP in Mississippi, the Hensons' daughter, Andrea Gibbs, led a successful campaign to close the Jones County jail down. (It's back in business, though.)

Camp Sister Spirit was created as a feminist and progressive education retreat. The Camp is utterly sober: chemically, psychologically, and politically. The women are security-conscious—they have to be. Like nuns, they patrol the property in pairs, and communicate with walkie-talkies. Camp Sister Spirit has been forced, very much against their will, to build a fence around the property. ("We could have fed 100 families for ten years with the money the fence is costing us?", Wanda Henson says.) Everyone knows where everyone else is. The women are legally armed. It's scary, isn't it, when women really start loving themselves enough to draw boundaries, defend their bodies, minds and way of life from attack.

Questions abound. Why should the feminist-government-in-exile choose Jones County, the historical heart of the Klan, as it's first outpost on earth? Why build a future where you're not wanted? (Tell that to the Israelis and the Palestinians). "Why not in Mississippi—the poorest state in the nation, and the most oppressed," Wanda says. "It's where I was born, it's where I'm from." Anyway where, exactly, are radical lesbian feminists wanted—and is land as cheap there (120 acres for $60,000) as in Ovett, Mississippi?

I ask: "Are you afraid?" "Absolutely," Brenda says. Wanda tells me about her trips to San Salvador and Mexico to help women and children. On one occasion, most volunteers had canceled making the trip out of fear. The organizer, who'd been previously tortured and imprisoned in San Salvador said to Wanda: "Sister, fear has no place here."

Wanda can thicken her southern accent until it becomes thick as the sweetest syrup and I'm tasting it and it's making me giddy. The only time that tears interrupted Wanda's high-spirited flow was when she told me that "black bodies still float down the Mississippi rivers. Where are they coming from? Who's killed them?" she asks, and she cried for others, not for herself.

Brenda and Wanda met on January 15, 1985, defending an abortion clinic in Pascagoula. Each had been married at 16, quickly had two children, and then fled violent husbands. Brenda had vowed that "if I ever got away from this fool and got some place safe that I would devote time and energy to the battered women's movement." Wanda was also battered—by a man and by one lesbian lover, and lost (but regained) custody of her children for being a lesbian. Brenda and Wanda legally took the single name of Brenda's supportive mother: Henson.

When the Hensons decided to buy land, with the help of a grant from Lesbian Natural Resources, they sought to establish a place of refuge, not confrontation. Harassment, however, has been persistent: a 9mm bullet hole tore through their mailbox; two sanitary napkins and a dead female puppy shot through the stomach were draped across their mailbox; ; they received a stream of threatening phone calls and letters and bomb threats; shots were fired at their front gate, roofing tacks placed on their roads (with 8 tires flattened as a result); their American and rainbow flags were torn down; intruders kept appearing on their property, low-flying planes took photos. "The local shopkeepers won't sell to us, or they charge us two to three times the going rate for something," Brenda said. A local lesbian supporter's house was mysteriously burned down three weeks ago. One caller warned: "expect the KKK to burn a cross on you."

Combatting violent, visible racism is part of what Camp Sister Spirit is about. (The Hensons conduct a Passover seder every year partly because they're entranced by it's vision of freedom—and as their way of taking a stand against anti-semitism.) Until the media 'discovered' Ovett, one drinking fountain outside the local courthouse was painted white, the other black. Overnight, both were painted white. The first time the Hensons, Pam, and Shirley, believed the death-threats might be real, they put out a call for help, Ben Chaney (yes, the brother of murdered civil rights worker James Chaney) came and spent the long night with them.

The media descended on Ovett in November of 1993. By mid-February or 1994, Attorney General Janet Reno had directed the Department of Justice to mediate the situation. The Hensons were thrilled that Janet Reno's mediators both turned out to be African-Americans; they thought this was ironic, a comeuppance, a measure of progress—and they also wondered, wearily, if that had contributed to making the mediation impossible. ("But who'd better understand how things are in Mississippi but an African-American, someone who comes from the state?", Wanda said.) In a letter to the

National Gay and Lesbian Task Force, Reno wrote "The intolerance and bigotry demonstrated by some of the people of Ovett have no place in this country." It was likely the first time in which federal mediators have been called into deal with violence directed at homosexuals.

Ironically, understandably, despite everything they know, the Camp is also trying to work 'within the system'. They've turned to the National Gay and Lesbian Task Force, to local lawyers, and to the Center for Constitutional Rights, the Lambda Legal Defense Fund, the National Center for Lesbian Rights, and to the Justice Department. But Camp Sister Spirit is totally without protection—and is prohibited, by both law and custom, from arming itself. Everyone at Camp Sister Spirit knows they exist in "No-Man's land" where, although the law may punish them for trying to protect themselves, (they cannot carry loaded firearms anywhere but on their own property), the law—including the FBI, may not be able to protect them or punish their persecutors. (The fact that FBI agents were still active in conducting an investigation into the death-threats, attempted shootings, and other intimidation, and the existence of several, ongoing lawsuits, may partially explain the absence of further or greater violence).

"The Hensons are feminists who happen to be lesbians," Lucy tells me. "Their deeds speak for them. Despite everything, calls for food, and for help with abuse are starting to come in. A grandmother gave her pregnant 14 year old granddaughter the number here." Gifts of tools, machine-parts, vegetables or other staples are made surreptitiously; local, especially local black supporters, have chosen to remain anonymous lest they suffer reprisals. (This year's Memorial Day Festival drew women from 18 states, all white. Women of color who'd attended before felt their presence would put themselves and the camp at even greater risk.)

Sasha tells me that the Hensons' son Arthur, who is 20, and "incredibly hard-working and loyal", is the only man who permanently lives on the land. "He left to make the Festival an all-woman space." Sasha also says that other men, including a friend of hers from Pittsburgh, have come to help. "What we're doing is for a principle. The Camp's outreach to the poor infuriates the locals. I've always stood up for what I believe in. If harm came to anyone, it wouldn't scare anyone away. We'd be right back there. The fences signal that we're here to stay. We're not going to back down." Sasha also points out that, in the ten miles stretch between the towns of Petal and Ovett, there are about 16 churches. "Local lesbian support isn't that good. A lotta the dykes and fags are Republicans in the closet." Brenda says that the local folk, who most stand to gain from the Camp's presence in the community, are being lied to and stirred up by "outside agitators" sent in by the Baptist Church.

That the Hensons—and their valiant volunteer supporters face danger daily can neither be denied nor exaggerated. The extraordinary willingness of so many presumably 'ordinary' and life-loving American women of all ages to share the Camp's fate is what's newsworthy. The fact that thousands more haven't been able to set aside their apathy, or narcissism, or terror, is old news. Camp Sister Spirit has received thousands of letters of support, (from both women and men who live in every state in the union, and in Europe and Asia too); they've received donations, and volunteers. This is nothing less than a miracle.

Nevertheless, at the recent Gay Pride March in New York City, men said to the Hensons: "Kick ass, right on, and here's my donation." There were exceptions, but women said: "Why is the Camp courting such danger? Why not retreat to some safer place? That would be nice, but women are always in danger: in our homes, on the street, at work. As we're picked off, one by one, most other women (and men) deny that things are that bad, or they look the other way when women, themselves included, are humiliated, harassed, cut down to size, overworked, underpaid, raped, beaten or killed. Refusing to become conscious about one's oppression doesn't make you safe; it just keeps you confused about what's happening to you."

At Camp Sister Spirit, the women are very conscious of danger: their own, and all women's everywhere. They've chosen to face the danger together, collectively. At Camp Sister Spirit, no one will die by her own hand, and no death will go unmourned or misunderstood.

As Wanda told me: "A woman at the farmer's market put her hands on me and stood real close to me and said, 'Honey, what's your name?' I told her my name was Wanda Henson. She said, 'I thought so. This doesn't have anything to do with the fact that you're different.' I asked her what she was talking about. She said 'What's happening to you has to do with the fact that you're a woman. Look. I've been living in Ovett for 53 years and I'm a woman land owner and I still have men coming on my property. Keep doing what you're doing because you're doing it for all of us."

Index

Index

Index

Index

Index

Index

Index

Smith, Hazel Brannon, 164
Smith, Ruby Doris, 164
Smith, William Kennedy, 110, 111
Son-of-Sam law, 124
Sons of Silence, 104
Sorkow, Judge Harvey, 41-42, 44, 45
Southern Poverty Law Center, 115, 122
Sovereign feminist government, 13
Speakouts, 63
Spillman, Dr. Emil, 110
Stanton, Elizabeth Cady, 22
Starr, Margaret, 21
State v. Wanrow, 116-123
Steinberg, Joel, 88
Steinem, gloria, 59
Stern, Betsy, 11
Stern, Melissa, 40-42
Stern, William, 11, 38, 40-45, 88
The St. John's Law Review, 8
Stone, Elizabeth T., 16, 19
Strong Mothers, Weak Wives, 54
Suffragists, 37-38
Suicide, 68-69
Supreme Court Gender Bias Report, 99
Supreme Court of Washington, 116-123
Surrogate parenting, 11, 35-36, 44-45

T

Tailhook scandal, 10
Tanner, John, 105, 112
"Temporary insanity" defense, 122
Terminator 2, 93
Thelma and Louise, 92 115
Thomas, Clarence, 55
Thomas (Shirley Mae) v. State, 120-121
Till, Emmett, 164
Truth, Sojourner, 164
Tubman, Harriet, 64
Tyson, Mike, 110

U

Underground railway, 64
"Uterus envy," 48

V

Vaginal Politics, 68
Validators, 82
Van den Ven, Nicole, 93
"Victim feminists," 63
Violence, 97-105, 168-169

W

Wachtler, Chief Justice Sol, 88
The Wanderground, 93
Walker, Lenore, 93, 123
Wallerstein, Dr. Judith, 53-54
Wanrow, Yvonne, 115-123
  crime of, 116-118
Warren, Judge William P., 77, 80
The Weekend, 94
Weir, Dr. S. Mitchell, 20

179

About the Author

Phyllis Chesler was active in the civil rights movement in the early 1960s and in the radical feminist movement from 1967 on. Since then she has lectured and organized political and legal campaigns all over the world, and has written many articles and six books, including *Women and Madness, Women, Money and Power* and *Sacred Bond: The Legacy of Baby M.* Now on leave from her professorship at the College of Staten Island at the City University of New York, she is editor-at-large for *On the Issues* Magazine.